D1546259

# THE ORIGIN AND DEVELOPMENT
## OF THE HOLY EUCHARIST: EAST AND WEST

# THE ORIGIN AND DEVELOPMENT OF THE HOLY EUCHARIST: EAST AND WEST

Andrew J. Gerakas, D.Min., Deacon

ST PAULS

# Alba
# House

Library of Congress Cataloging-in-Publication Data

Gerakas, Andrew J.
    The origin and development of the Holy Eucharist, East and West / Andrew J. Gerakas.
        p. cm.
    Includes bibliographical references.
    ISBN 0-8189-1228-6
    1. The Lord's Supper—Catholic Church—History.    2. Lord's Supper—Orthodox Eastern
Church—History.    3. Catholic Church—Relations—Orthodox Eastern Church. 4. Orthodox
Eastern Church—Relations—Catholic Church.    I. Title.

BV823.G39 2006
234'.16309—dc22

                            2005032193

Produced and designed in the United States of America by the
Fathers and Brothers of the Society of St. Paul,
2187 Victory Boulevard, Staten Island, New York 10314-6603,
as part of their communications apostolate.


ISBN: 0-8189-1228-6
ISBN: 978-0-8189-1228-3

**Printing Information:**

| Current Printing - first digit | 1 | 2 | 3 | 4 | 5 | 6 | 7 | 8 | 9 | 10 |
|---|---|---|---|---|---|---|---|---|---|---|

Year of Current Printing - first year shown

| 2006 | 2007 | 2008 | 2009 | 2010 | 2011 | 2012 | 2013 | 2014 | 2015 |
|---|---|---|---|---|---|---|---|---|---|

# TABLE OF CONTENTS

# PREFACE

As an eight-year-old I sat frightened on the knee of Athenagoras, who was then Orthodox Archbishop of North and South America of the Greek Orthodox Church. He later became the Ecumenical Patriarch of the worldwide Orthodox Church. I had just recited a poem, in Greek, before the entire school, with parents and teachers attending the end of the Greek school year at Holy Trinity Cathedral in New York. Athenagoras was six feet four inches tall with a long beard and a deep voice. He congratulated me on my performance and gave me his blessing but I just wanted to get away from that giant and go to my mother. The scene is indelible in my memory. Athenagoras was later to become a key figure in reconciliation efforts between the Eastern and Western Churches.

I was blessed with devout Greek Orthodox immigrant parents, who came from the northern Aegean island of Lemnos, but whose marriage was arranged, as was the custom in those days, in New York. We had to go to Greek school after regular school. In our case, my sister and I who were eight and seven when we started, had to take the Third Avenue elevated train from the South Bronx to the Cathedral in Manhattan on our own. When we returned we had to do both our English and Greek homework. You can imagine how we felt since our fellow classmates would go out to play after American school while we had to take the train downtown. Our Greek teachers and priests would tell us that we would be sorry if we did not concentrate on our work.

I didn't, and I am sorry. I remember the very pale young Greek deacon who taught us. He passed away, apparently from cancer, and I often wonder whether he prayed for me, since some forty-five years later, I became a deacon in the Roman Catholic Church.

I have fond memories of Greek school, beautiful and inspiring liturgies and church related socials. My parents were immigrants trying to make their way in a new land, beset by an economic depression they did not understand, but persevering gallantly with strong family ties and deep ethnic loyalty.

We were also blessed to have been able to move to the upper Bronx into a largely Orthodox Jewish neighborhood. I was impressed with the dedication of the Jewish people to their religion, their friendliness, and their complete acceptance of us and we of them. Here we shared the common problem of a deep economic depression, which brought us all closer to each other. We lived on the fifth floor of our apartment building next to the Feigenbaums who became our lifelong friends. I still feel a sense of gratitude to the devout Jewish women, for whom I lit gas jets on their Sabbath, starting on the ground floor and working my way up to the fifth floor. In turn, I received a few pennies and, sometimes, a nickel. I saved this money until I had fifty-five cents, waited for a double header, and walked the seven or eight miles to Yankee Stadium, sitting on a bleacher bench under the hot sun. A WPA (Works Projects Administration) pool and Crotona Park were just across the street. We played and swam together. I consider our stay in the Jewish neighborhood, the golden age of my youth.

A longing to receive the Lord in the Holy Eucharist on a daily basis was the primary reason for my becoming a Roman Catholic, although I have never felt that I left the Orthodox Church. During the early years of my residency in Honolulu, there was no Orthodox Church.

Each person's background and experiences influence their beliefs and aspirations. My experience in the Jewish community has given me an open mind to better understand the importance of the Jewish legacy in Christian belief and practices. My Greek background has encouraged an interest in the contribution of the early Greek Fathers to Christian theology and its relation to the Eucharist. My daily prayer at the Eucharistic table is that the Churches of the East and West once again "break bread" together at the same table of the Lord.

I dedicate this publication to Eugene La Verdiere, SSS, a Blessed Sacrament Father and Scripture scholar, who encouraged me to research this topic and to write on the Holy Eucharist.

# INTRODUCTION

The Eucharist is Jesus Christ's gift to His followers to sustain them lest they faint along the way as they journey to their eternal home. As a sacrament, it is a visible sign of His abiding presence, body, blood, soul and divinity in our midst under the appearance of bread and wine. Our physical nature, made up as it is of flesh as well as spirit needs such a visible sign to sustain it, and the Lord provides this sign through these two common elements in which He makes Himself present.

The source and summit of the Church's life and mission is to be found in the celebration of the liturgy. The Eucharist is not celebrated and lived in isolation but is brought into the world by the recipient as a life-giving force. It nourishes us so that we may have life and have it to the full and it enables us to bring that life to others through our love. It gives us the strength to discipline ourselves, to resist temptations against our weaknesses from within as well as from without, and to reach out to those in need as Jesus did. Through the Eucharist Jesus dwells in the humble recipient of Holy Communion. His indwelling presence invites an imitation of Himself in the faithful person's individual life and circumstances.

In Holy Communion Christians of the East and West receive the body, blood, soul and divinity of Christ. But what does this mean? Do we receive Jesus of Nazareth: the carpenter, the teacher, the healer? Do we not also receive the suffering and crucified Jesus? When we receive the Eucharist we partake of the banquet of the Kingdom. It is not only the historical Jesus Who is present but also the resurrected Lord, the ascended Lord and the Lord Who is King of heaven and earth and all of God's creation. We get a taste of heaven here on earth. At the appointed time, our bodies will be resurrected to join our souls because our very bones and sinews have been fed with Him Who lives forever at the right hand of the Father. Ours will be a glorified body that will never decay. The chapter on Theosis delves into this mystery.

How can we, Christians of the East and West, receive the Lord worthily? What must we bring to the altar? The Lord gives Himself completely and unadulteratedly to us. Should we not also give ourselves completely and unadulteratedly to Him? In the sacrament of love Jesus gives us Himself entirely and gratuitously. As responding lovers should we not also give ourselves entirely and gratuitously? There will not be a complete fusion of love if Jesus gives Himself completely while we only give ourselves partly. The union of ourselves with Jesus in the sacrament of love is not just a private affair between the communicant and the Lord, providing us with nourishment for both body and soul. It is likewise (a) the offering of ourselves in union with all others of the pilgrim Church on earth, (b) the offering of the entire assembly to Jesus as a community, and (c) the uniting of the earthly Church with our high priest Jesus Christ, leading us, in union with the heavenly Church, as one holy oblation to God the Father of love.

The pilgrim Church and the heavenly Church are brought together with and through Jesus, in union with the Holy Spirit, as one holy oblation to the Father of love. With this fusion of love we are united with the Holy Trinity, our ultimate and eternal destiny. In this sense we are already united here, as one Church, through the action of the Lord, our high priest. Just as there is one holy oblation to the Father, the earthly Church should continually seek to grow in fraternal love and unity.

The Eucharist is unifying because when we receive the Lord, as we should, we enter more deeply into our relationship with Him as His brothers and sisters. Yet there is a division between the Church of the East and the Church of the West. While the two Churches do not celebrate the Eucharist together there is a recognition of the legitimacy of each other's celebrations. The two no longer live in isolation. Modern communications, joint theological discussions, and annual celebrations of St. Peter and St. Paul and St. Andrew contribute to a better understanding of each other.

Both Churches have a strong devotion to the Blessed Virgin Mary, Panaghia, the "all holy one." It is she who brought forth Jesus. She is the Theotokos, the mother of God, the mother of Him Who is present in the Eucharist. She is also the mother of all the faithful in the order of grace. Mothers always seek to bring peace and unity within the family. She teaches by example. Her heart was so open, so humble, so ready to do the Lord's will, that the Almighty overshadowed her, and she conceived the God/man by the power of the Holy Spirit. Christians of the East and West continually ask her, who gave our Lord His body and blood, and Whose divinity also passed through her, to have a humble ready soul to receive our Lord worthily. Just as He was fashioned in the womb of Mary, the all holy one, we too, are mysteriously fashioned into His likeness.

How the Churches of the East and the West, who claim the same holy mother, prepare for, gather, and consume their heavenly bread is explored in these pages. Accordingly, some of the commonly accepted biblical background for the Eucharist will be reviewed, as also the history and evolution of Holy Communion in the Orthodox and Roman Catholic Churches, and a comparison will be made of current practices.

Often we do not realize enough how much we owe others for our celebrations and our theology. The chapters on our Jewish and Greek heritage seek to expose, for our better understanding, the debt we owe, first of all, to our Jewish brethren, who are our spiritual ancestors, and then to the early Greek Fathers, who developed our basic theology and understanding of Jesus and His presence in the Eucharist.

Also reviewed will be some of the basic doctrinal and organizational differences that inhibit a return to intercommunion, the ultimate goal of both Churches, and to fulfill the Lord's prayer that all may be one.

# Biblical Abbreviations

## OLD TESTAMENT

| | | | | | |
|---|---|---|---|---|---|
| Genesis | Gn | Nehemiah | Ne | Baruch | Ba |
| Exodus | Ex | Tobit | Tb | Ezekiel | Ezk |
| Leviticus | Lv | Judith | Jdt | Daniel | Dn |
| Numbers | Nb | Esther | Est | Hosea | Ho |
| Deuteronomy | Dt | 1 Maccabees | 1 M | Joel | Jl |
| Joshua | Jos | 2 Maccabees | 2 M | Amos | Am |
| Judges | Jg | Job | Jb | Obadiah | Ob |
| Ruth | Rt | Psalms | Ps | Jonah | Jon |
| 1 Samuel | 1 S | Proverbs | Pr | Micah | Mi |
| 2 Samuel | 2 S | Ecclesiastes | Ec | Nahum | Na |
| 1 Kings | 1 K | Song of Songs | Sg | Habakkuk | Hab |
| 2 Kings | 2 K | Wisdom | Ws | Zephaniah | Zp |
| 1 Chronicles | 1 Ch | Sirach | Si | Haggai | Hg |
| 2 Chronicles | 2 Ch | Isaiah | Is | Malachi | Ml |
| Ezra | Ezr | Jeremiah | Jr | Zechariah | Zc |
| | | Lamentations | Lm | | |

## NEW TESTAMENT

| | | | | | |
|---|---|---|---|---|---|
| Matthew | Mt | Ephesians | Eph | Hebrews | Heb |
| Mark | Mk | Philippians | Ph | James | Jm |
| Luke | Lk | Colossians | Col | 1 Peter | 1 P |
| John | Jn | 1 Thessalonians | 1 Th | 2 Peter | 2 P |
| Acts | Ac | 2 Thessalonians | 2 Th | 1 John | 1 Jn |
| Romans | Rm | 1 Timothy | 1 Tm | 2 John | 2 Jn |
| 1 Corinthians | 1 Cor | 2 Timothy | 2 Tm | 3 John | 3 Jn |
| 2 Corinthians | 2 Cor | Titus | Tt | Jude | Jude |
| Galatians | Gal | Philemon | Phm | Revelation | Rv |

# THE ORIGIN AND DEVELOPMENT
# OF THE HOLY EUCHARIST: EAST AND WEST

# I

# THE LOGOS

We begin with this chapter on the Logos because the Word provides the necessary preparation for receiving the Lord in the Eucharist. The Logos, the Word, prepares and cultivates the soil of our soul before planting that which brings forth life and growth.

> In the beginning was the Word
> and the Word was with God,
> and the Word was God....
> And the Word became flesh
> and made His dwelling among us,
> and we saw His glory,
> the glory as of the Father's only Son,
> full of grace and of truth. (Jn 1:1, 14)

The Logos became flesh and dwelt among us so that we can dwell with Him and, through Him and with Him, live with the Father forever. "I pray not only for them but also for those who will believe in Me through their word, so that they may all be one, as You, Father, are in Me and I in You, that they also may be one in Us" (Jn 17:20). The Logos is more than a simple vocal utterance; it is the very self-communication of God Himself.

The term "Logos" has a variety of meanings. Words have a

way of developing so as to more precisely connote human thought. "Logos" is a common term in Greek philosophical thought. Heraclitus (500 BCE), the Greek philosopher, used it in the sense of a universal reason governing and permeating the world. It became popular in Stoic philosophical thinking and when it reached Alexandria was given a Platonic flavor as an intermediary between God and the world.

Philo (20-50 CE), the great Jewish philosopher and interpreter of the Scriptures, connected the Logos with the genesis of the world and life, signifying through it the act of creation and giving it an almost personal identity as an intermediary between God and the world. He used the term over a thousand times. It is used in the Greek translation of the Psalms, for example Ps 107:20, "He sent forth His word to heal them and to snatch them from destruction…," and Ps 119:130, "The unfolding of Your words give light; it imparts understanding to the simple."

In the Christian Scriptures "Logos" is found in the Prologue of John's Gospel (above). Following the Prologue, which refers to the pre-existence of the Second Person of the Blessed Trinity, John's Gospel uses the term "Son of Man," and less frequently, "Son of God" to refer to Jesus.

"Logos," however, reappears in the First Epistle of John: "What was from the beginning, what we have heard, what we have seen with our eyes, what we looked upon and touched with our hands concerns the **Word** of life…" (1 Jn 1; emphasis added); and in Revelation: "The revelation of Jesus Christ, which God gave Him to show to His servants what must soon take place… He made known by sending His angel to His servant John, who bore witness to the **word** of God and to the testimony of Jesus Christ…" (Rv 1:1, 2; emphasis added). Biblical scholars believe that John's use and meaning of the term "Logos" is not related to philosophical literature but to Jewish Scripture, rhetoric and imagery of God's Word.

The summit of the Church's worship of God is to be found in the Holy Sacrifice of the Mass, and the centrality of the Mass is the Eucharist. Preceding the Eucharist is the Liturgy of the Word, the spoken word and Logos, the very self of Christ, that is bonded to the uttered word. The word without Christ is without life. The word with Christ imbeds itself and where it finds fertile soil yields one hundred, sixty and thirtyfold (Mk 4:8). Before Jesus introduced the Eucharist He tilled the spiritual soil with the spoken word so that the Eucharist might find fertile ground. The word and the Eucharist are inseparable but the word must necessarily precede the Eucharist.

The Logos contains the power and dynamism of God's creativity (Gn 1). The words, "Then God said," precede each of His creative acts. The Word is spoken and creation comes into being. By His Logos He creates. God is always at the heart of each thing maintaining it in being: "God looked at everything He had made, and He found it very good" (Gn 1:31). While God is in all things He cannot be contained in anything. While God pervades everything, He is not everything — pantheism. He is beyond and above all things. God redeems and renews. He spoke directly to Moses and revealed Himself through the prophets. He is the heart of the life of every human being. In the Christian Scriptures Jesus is the very Word of God incarnate. His proclamation is also referred to as the word of God (Lk 5:1), as is His prophetic vocation (Mt 12:41; Mk 6:4), His power to exorcize, and to heal (Mt 8:16).

The early Church Fathers such as Justin the Martyr (d. 165) and Irenaeus (d. 200) developed the term further. The Logos mediated creation and revelation. For Justin God's Reason, incarnate in Christ, is also the diffused Reason that speaks in every person. He adopted the term familiar to the Stoics of the "spermatic word," the divine force impregnating the universe (*Second Apology*, 10, 13; Richardson, 233). "We have been taught that Christ is the First-begotten of God, and have previously testified that He is the Reason of which every race of man partakes. Those who lived in accordance with Reason are Christians, even though they were called godless, such as among the Greeks, Socrates and Heraclitus. ... But those who live by Reason, and those who so now live are Christians, fearless and unperturbed. For what cause a man was conceived of a virgin by the power of the **Word** according to the will of God, the Father and Master of all, and was named Jesus... an intelligent man will be able to comprehend from the words that were spoken in various ways" (*First Apology*, 46; Ibid., 272, emphasis added).

Justin emphasized that creation is the work of the supreme God, acting through the Logos as mediator; that in the Incarnation the Logos assumed a complete manhood, body, soul and mind, and Christ "truly suffered in His passion; above all that the destiny of man hereafter is not a deliverance of an immortal soul from the bondage of the physical frame, but is 'resurrection,'" which Justin interpreted in a most literal way (Chadwick, 77).

Irenaeus in polemic against Valentinus said, "the Son is 'produced' from the Father as a **word** is 'emitted' from the mind, or by human speech" (*Against Heresies* 2:28,6; O'Collins, 7/8/92, emphasis added). Irenaeus compared Adam with the new Adam, Jesus, and Eve with the new Eve, Mary. Mary was obedient to the **Word** while Eve was not: "For as Eve was seduced by the word of an angel to flee from God, having rebelled against his Word, so Mary by the word of an angel received the glad tidings that she would bear God by obeying his Word" (5:19; Richardson, 389).

Because of the need to fight heresies, maintain orthodoxy and discern the truth, a problem with the conceptual content of the Logos has been the threat of reducing the word "Logos" to an intellectual concept rather than to recognize the Logos as God's self-disclosure. In addition, the emphasis on the sacraments without the necessary groundwork of the Word led to an almost exclusive concentration on Scripture by Protestant scholars. The post-Vatican II emphasis on the study of Scripture has resulted in a tremendous surge in Catholic biblical scholarship. *Dei Verbum* (The Word of God), the Dogmatic Constitution on Divine Revelation promulgated by Vatican II returned to the biblical presentation of the Word of God as God's self-disclosure. It is personified in Jesus through the proclamation of the Word by the Church.

At the heart of an understanding of the Logos is the concept of human participation in God's own divine life. It was central to many of the theological disputes brought before the first five ecumenical councils on the nature of Jesus. The union of divinity and humanity in Christ allows our communion with the Logos. Eastern Orthodoxy would say, "Man is truly man when he participates in divine life and realizes in himself the image and likeness of God, and this participation in no way diminishes his authentically human existence, human energy and will" (Meyendorff, 210).

The term "Logos," as we have said, conveys more than the simple concept of an external vocalized word, although it certainly includes that. It is the self-revelation of God as personified in the Second Person of the Blessed Trinity, Jesus, the Word made flesh. Jesus, true God and true man, enables us to be united with Him through His manhood. This allows us to partake of His Godhead in union with Him while maintaining our distinct human nature. The resurrected Jesus enables us then to be resurrected with Him so that we may live in Him and, with Him and through Him, to live forever with the Father.

An aspect of the Logos that we want to emphasize here is the proclamation of the Word of God. The proclaimed Word gives growth where it finds fertile soil, for attached to that spoken Word is the self disclosure of God which is life-giving, fruitful and eternal. When the Word is properly proclaimed and adequately received it reveals the mind of God. The Word that is uttered is accompanied by the Spirit of the risen Christ. Said another way, Jesus is present when His Word is proclaimed.

The Lord utters the Word and His Word is truth. Jesus' response to Pilate was: "For this I was born and for this I came into the world to testify to the truth. Everyone who belongs to the truth listens to My voice" (Jn 18:37). Jesus testifies to the truth. His words can either be accepted or rejected:

> Everyone who listens to these words of Mine and acts on them will be like a wise man who built his house on rock. The rain fell, the floods came, and the winds blew and buffeted the house. But it did not collapse; it had been set solidly on rock. And everyone who listens to these words of Mine but does not act on them will be like a fool who built his house on sand. The rain fell, the floods came, and the wind blew and buffeted the house. And it collapsed and was completely ruined. (Mt 7:24-27)

The Word is the charisma of the Jewish prophet. It is a dynamic entity, an expansion of the living personality of Yahweh. Yahweh places His Word in the mouth of the prophet. The person of Yahweh invades, through the Word, the personality of the prophet. The prophet cannot contain himself but must proclaim the Word. Like the rain and the snow the Word does not return without accomplishing that for which it was sent (Is 55:10). It is eternal with the eternity of the will which it embodies (Is 40:8). The Word goes where it wills, lights on whom it wills, and enlightens whom it wills. Said another way, God loves all His creation and reveals Himself to whom He wills, when He wills and in the manner He wills.

With respect to participation in the Logos there is neither Jew nor Greek, male or female, rich or poor, slave or free. A reference to a famous Hellene would, perhaps, give an example. A serious accusation against Socrates during his trial was that he believed in one God. He claimed that God came to him even as a little boy and that he was following God's will (Plato, *Apology*, 27). Socrates believed in life after death (*Phaedo*). Perhaps he had an inkling of the one true God as somehow revealed to him. Observation would lead us to conclude that there is much beauty and truth in all people and in many religions. As in the case of Socrates the truth is somewhat clouded. Socrates sought the truth at any cost and Justin Martyr calls him a Christian because he lived by "reason" (*First Apology*, 46). Karl Rahner, as covered in the chapter on Theosis, would call him an "anonymous Christian."

In addition to "reason" or "mind" or "word," the Logos can mean "wisdom" (sophia). In the Book of Proverbs we find the following passage regarding the personification of wisdom: "The Lord begot me, the first-born of His ways.... From of old I was poured forth, at the first, before the earth.... When He established the heavens I was there.... When He made firm the skies above, when He fixed fast the foundations of the earth; When He set the sea its limit.... Then was I beside Him as His craftsman, and I was His delight day by day, Playing before Him all the while, playing on the surface of the earth; and I found delight in the sons of men" (8:22-31).

It is clear that the Logos shows no partiality. The Logos delights in all peoples. The Logos is Greek to the Greeks, Jewish to the Jews, Portuguese to the Portuguese, French to the French, Chinese to the Chinese. The Logos is all in all and for all.

The disciples of the risen Christ are formed by the Logos, the Word, which precedes the Holy Eucharist. They are made ready to receive the God/Man in Holy Communion. We have to thank our Semitic origins for the Liturgy of the Word. It is a Christianized version of the synagogue service with the reading of biblical passages, the homily and prayer. The early believers in Jesus prayed in the synagogue and followed the same pattern after they were ejected or left the synagogue.

The brilliant early Church Father Origen likened the Word to the Eucharist:

> I want to base my exhortation to you on examples drawn from your religious practices. You regularly attend the various mysteries, and you know how reverently and carefully you protect the Body of the Lord when it is given to you, for you fear a fragment of it may fall to the ground and part of the consecrated treasure be lost. If it did, you would regard yourselves as culpable, and rightly so, if through your negligence something of it were lost. Well, then, if you show such justifiable care when it comes to his Body, why should you think that neglect of God's word should deserve a lesser punishment than neglect of his Body. (*Homiliae in Exodum* 13:3; P. Jacquement, *The Eucharist of the Early Christians*, 183)

The Liturgy of the Word and the Eucharist are intimately related and are inseparable. In fact, the Liturgy of the Word constitutes an essential and most proper preparation for the Eucharist, because the Word of God has the power to judge, convert, purify, heal, and transform the lives of people, making them worthy of that which they are about to receive. "You are already cleansed because of the word which I have spoken to you.… He who abides in Me, and I in him, bears much fruit; for without Me you can do nothing.… If you abide in Me, and My words abide in you, you will ask what you desire and it shall be done for you" (Jn 15:3, 5, 7). Jesus equates the Word with truth. "I have given them Your word and the world has hated them because they do not belong to the world, just as I do not belong to the world.... Sanctify them in the truth; Your word is truth" (Jn 17:14, 17).

Jesus says that the words He utters are what the Father has commanded Him to say. The words that He has spoken have the power to condemn those who hear but do not observe them: "And if anyone hears My words and does not observe them, I do not condemn him, for I did not come to condemn the world but to save the world. Whoever rejects Me and does not accept My words has something to judge him: namely, the word that I spoke; it will condemn him on the last day, because I do not speak on My own, but the Father Who sent Me commanded Me what to say and speak. And I know that His commandment is eternal life. So what I say, I say as the Father told Me" (Jn 12:47-50).

The disciples of the risen Christ are to be extensions of the Logos, the Word. They are to be formed by the Word and given life by the Eucharist. Like Jesus they are to recognize the uniqueness of each person created by God in His own image and likeness. They are to transmit that Word in their own language and culture both by example, and, where appropriate, audibly, so that there is a better understanding of the wisdom and love of the Logos through Whom all are created, sustained, and receive everlasting life.

In referring to the sacrificial aspect of the Mass Pope Benedict XVI, as a Cardinal, said, "Therefore the sacrifice is effective where *His* word is heard, the word of the Word, by which He transformed His death into an event of meaning and of love, in order that we, through being able to take up His words for ourselves, are led onward into His love, onward into the love of the Trinity, in which He eternally hands Himself over to the Father. There, where the words of the Word ring forth, and our gifts thus become His gifts, through which He gives Himself, *that* is the sacrificial element that has ever and always been characteristic of the Eucharist" (Ratzinger, 66, 67).

The challenge to the disciples of the risen Christ is to "break the bread of the Word" distributing it with the presence of Jesus to those who have heard and to those who have not heard, for all are hungry for the Logos of life. After adequately receiving the Word their hunger will increase for the holy sacrament of the Eucharist.

And after the Eucharist the hunger, while temporarily satisfied for the journey, will not be satiated until we all sit down together at the heavenly banquet.

# II

# BIBLICAL EUCHARISTIC PREFIGUREMENT

## PREFIGUREMENT IN THE JEWISH SCRIPTURES

The Jewish Scriptures are replete with prefigurements of the Eucharist.

### Adam's Side — Jesus' Side

When God took one of Adam's ribs from his side to create Eve, Adam said of her that she was, "bone of my bones and flesh of my flesh." Just as Adam was in a deep sleep when God took the rib from his side (Gn 2:21), Jesus had given up His spirit (Jn 19:30) and was in the deep sleep of death when blood and water flowed from His side (19:34). Just as God took a rib from Adam's side to form Eve, so Christ gave us blood and water from His side to wash us clean, a prefigurement of Baptism, and blood from His side to give us life, a prefigurement of the Eucharist. Jesus gave himself completely, every drop of blood and water; nothing was held back. As a proof of His infinite love for us, He made the ultimate sacrifice of His life for our salvation. Just as a mother feeds her child with her own blood, so does Christ feed those whom He has begotten with His own blood.

## Abraham Offers Isaac — God Offers His Son

Abraham was willing to offer his son Isaac as a holocaust to God. God stayed his hand from slaughtering Isaac by having His angel say to him, "Do not lay your hand on the boy…. Do not do the least harm to him. I know how devoted you are to God since you did not withhold from Me **your only beloved son**" (Gn 22:11-12, emphasis added).

God stayed Abraham's hand but he allowed His **only beloved Son** to be offered as a holocaust for the salvation of the world (Mk 1:11, 9:7; Mt: 3:17, 17:5; Lk 3:22). Abraham was *willing* to give all but Christ *actually did* give all — everything, holding back nothing. He gave himself completely — every drop of blood and water to God the Father for the sake of His people. Abraham's willingness to sacrifice his beloved son opened the way for God the Father to offer His only Son since God cannot be outdone in generosity and love. Since the natural concomitant of love is a willingness to sacrifice, to give all, God could not be outdone in His willingness to sacrifice. It is that same sacrifice that is offered in the Eucharistic celebration.

## Blood on the Doorposts Saves the Jews — Christ's Blood Saves Us

Christ's blood is also foreshadowed in the Exodus drama. Moses told his people on the night before they were to leave Egypt to sacrifice a lamb without blemish and to sprinkle the lintel and door posts of their homes with its blood. The angel of death passed over and did not strike any of the homes of the Jews, not so much because it was the blood of a lamb but because that blood prefigured the precious blood of Christ, the unblemished Lamb of God (Ex 12:21-23). Indeed, John the Baptist would later identify Jesus as "the Lamb of God" (Jn 1:36).

Just as the blood of the sacrificed Passover lamb assured the safe passage and deliverance of the Jews from their oppressive bondage in Egypt, so does the blood of Christ, the true Lamb of God, given to us in the Eucharist, save us from the slavery of sin and death.

### Joseph, a Prefigure of Christ Who Feeds the World

Joseph the favorite son of Israel (Jacob) was a prefigure of Christ. He wore a long tunic made for him by his father. Jesus wore a seamless tunic most probably made for Him by His holy mother. Joseph was thrown in a cistern by his brothers. Jesus was placed in the bowels of the earth for three days. Joseph was lifted out of the cistern. Jesus was raised from the tomb. Joseph was sold for 20 pieces of silver. Jesus was sold for 30 pieces of silver.

"All the world came to Joseph to obtain rations of grain, for famine had gripped the whole world" (Gn 41:57). Jacob sent his sons to Joseph to seek food because of the famine everywhere. Israel then migrated to Egypt, "with all that was his" as God had directed him. "Do not be afraid to go down to Egypt for there I will make you a great nation" (Gn 46:3). Today the whole world hungers for God and Jesus feeds all those who come to Him with the finest wheat, "the bread of life."

Joseph, the favored son of Israel, and the one blessed by God, is a prefigure of Jesus, the only begotten Son of God, Who feeds the hungry with His body and blood.

### Manna From Heaven — The Bread of Life

In the desert the whole Israelite community grumbled against Moses and Aaron and said to them, "Would that we had died at the Lord's hand in the land of Egypt as we sat by our flesh pots and ate our fill of bread. But you had to lead us into this desert to make the whole community die of famine." (Ex 16:2, 3)

The Lord spoke to Moses, "I have heard the grumbling of the Israelites. Tell them, in the evening twilight you shall eat flesh, and in the morning you shall have your fill of bread, so that you may know that I, the Lord am your God." (Ex 16:11, 12)

And so it came about. In the evening quail came up and covered the camp and, when the dew evaporated, there on the surface of the desert were fine flakes like hoarfrost on the ground. On seeing it the Israelites asked one another, "What is this?" for they did not know what it was. But Moses told them, "This is the bread which the Lord has given you to eat." (Ex 16:13-15)

The Israelites called this food manna. It was like coriander seed, but white and it tasted like wafers made with honey. (Ex 16:31)

The Israelites ate this manna for forty years, until they came to settled land; they ate manna until they reached the borders of Canaan. (Ex 16:35)

Since early Christian times, the manna has been considered a prefigurement of the bread of the Eucharist. The Jews ate manna until they reached the Promised Land. The sojourn in the desert by the Jews is also a prefigurement of the Christian's trek in this world. The Promised Land for the Christian is heaven. In the meantime the Christian sojourns in an arid wasteland on earth and his soul yearns for God. The Christian is a stranger in this world. He is merely passing through. The Christian who longs for his God is a temporary resident, a resident alien of this earth. During his difficult journey, the Christian is sustained by the "real bread from heaven," the Holy Eucharist, lest he faint along the way (Mt 15:32).

Our Lord referred to Himself as the "real bread from heaven." The crowd challenged Jesus to perform a sign saying, "Our ancestors had manna to eat in the desert; according to Scripture, 'He gave them bread from the heavens to eat.'" In reply, Jesus said to them:

> I solemnly assure you, it was not Moses who gave you bread from the heavens; it is My Father Who gives you the real heavenly bread. God's bread comes down from heaven and gives life to the world. I Myself am the bread of life. No one who comes to Me shall ever be hungry, no one who believes in Me shall ever thirst. (Jn 6:31-33, 35)

When Christians offer themselves to God and partake of Him in the Eucharist, they are receiving heaven's food — the "bread of life come down from heaven for the salvation of the world." This food sustains them as they journey through the desert of life until they reach their heavenly home. Then they will be strangers no longer, for God the Father will not be outdone in hospitality. In His home there are many mansions.

## The Psalms and the Holy Eucharist

The 150 psalms of the Hebrew Scriptures speak of the love of God for His people and a careful look at them reveals the longing of the Lord to feed us with Himself.

## Psalm 110

> The Lord has sworn and He will not repent, You are
> a priest forever according to the order of Melchizedek.
> (v. 4)

Melchizedek, who was a king of Salem, offered God bread
and wine and as a priest he blessed Abram (Gn 14:18). Jesus offered up bread and wine together with Himself and that sacrificial
offering is what we receive in Holy Communion. In the Letter
to the Hebrews the reference by God to Jesus is, "You are a priest
forever according to the order of Melchizedek" (Heb 5:6; 7:17).
In the sacrifice of the Mass, Jesus, the high priest, makes the ultimate offering of His body and blood which we receive in the
form of bread and wine.

## Psalm 107

In Psalm 107 the Lord rescues His people who have gone
astray in the wilderness, i.e., in the world (v. 4) and like a good
shepherd He fills them with **good things** (v. 9). God overshadowed the Blessed Virgin Mary and with His Holy Spirit formed
Jesus in her. He makes His abode with her and she proclaims in
her Canticle:

> The hungry He has given every **good thing**. (Lk 1:53;
> emphasis added)

Mary tells us that those who hunger for the Lord will be
given the finest food, His body and blood in the Holy Eucharist.

## Psalm 78

He rained manna upon them for food and gave them heavenly bread. The bread of the mighty was eaten by men. (78:24, 25a)

When we eat the bread from heaven we must do it with worthy hearts dedicated to God's will. Otherwise God's anger will rise against us (v. 31) and the manna will lead to trials. We must not be like the Corinthians whom St. Paul admonished because of the way they conducted themselves at their agape meal and Eucharistic celebration. We must recognize Jesus in the breaking of the bread and give due reverence to the presence of God in our midst (1 Cor 11:17-23).

## Psalms 81 and 35

Palm 81 carries on with the same theme. If we do not listen to the Lord's voice and obey Him, He will give us up to the hardness of our hearts. But if we hear Him and walk in His ways, (Ps 81:12-14) then we can open wide our mouths and He will fill us with the best of wheat and with honey from the rock (Ps 81:17). Rock is a title for Yahweh. The food from the rock is the food from God — the Holy Eucharist. Taste and see how good the Lord is (Ps 34:9). And after you have tasted, you will see that the Lord is good (1 P 2:3).

## Psalm 23

You have prepared a table before me in the sight of my foes. (Ps 23:5)

The Lord's table contains heavenly food and our foes include not only adversaries but the world and its sirens. We come to the Eucharist as to an oasis in the midst of the arid land around us. We are strengthened by this heavenly food to persevere with fortitude until we reach the Promised Land.

## Psalms 145, 42, 63, 134

"The eyes of all look hopefully to God and He gives them their food in due time" (Ps 145:15). Like exiles we pray to be delivered from our enemies and to be restored to the presence of our Savior and our God (Ps 42:12). Like David in the wilderness of Judah, our flesh pines and our souls thirst for God; to gaze on Him in the sanctuary and to see His power and glory (Ps 63:1-3). "Even during the hours of the night, we lift up our hands toward the sanctuary and bless the Lord" (Ps 134:1b, 2).

The excerpts from the foregoing psalms suggest the adoration of the Lord in His sanctuary, including nocturnal adoration and benediction. It prefigures adoration and prayer before the Eucharist and receiving Him spiritually into our souls as we pray in the presence of the Holy Eucharist.

Both the Orthodox and Catholic Churches believe that all the Jewish Scriptures are important and should be studied and pondered — all lead to Jesus and the unfolding of God's salvific plan.

The Jewish Scriptures sing of the love of God for us, His willingness to sacrifice His only-begotten Son for our salvation, and, that He will feed us with the finest wheat, the bread from heaven, on our journey to Him.

## PREFIGUREMENT IN THE CHRISTIAN SCRIPTURES

The Christian Scriptures were written to be proclaimed to the various Christian communities and each evangelist fashioned the proclaimed message to fit his audience and its needs. To this end and to the extent that each of them sought to emphasize certain aspects of the Lord's message, as unique individuals their interpretations varied, so the Christian Scriptures differ. The basic message, however, is always the same: the love of God for each and every one of the human beings He created, His desire to redeem them all, and His determination to spare nothing in His love and effort.

**The "Our Father"**

The "Our Father" was recited by Christians as a preparation for Holy Communion before it became part of the liturgy. Only the baptized qualified to receive the Eucharist were allowed to say it. In the early Christian communities it was a secret prayer. It was said before the "breaking of the bread" (Holy Communion). This basic prayer was taught us by the Lord Himself when His disciples asked Him to teach them how to pray in Luke's Gospel. In Matthew's Gospel, as a part of the Sermon on the Mount, Jesus recommends this prayer to all His followers. The request in this prayer for "our daily bread" will be the focus here.

Give us each day our daily bread... (Lk 11:3)
Give us this day our daily bread... (Mt 6:11)

This is the common English translation. As the Christian Scriptures come to us from the Greek, a literal translation of Luke's version would go something like, "The bread of us belonging to the morrow give us each day." St. Jerome reportedly found an Aramaic version of the Lord's Prayer which translated refers to "the bread of tomorrow." In Matthew it is, "The bread of us daily give to us." During Jesus' time bread was the principal part of the meal and the term was often used to describe the entire meal.

The Greek word used in the Lord's Prayer is "epiousion" which modern translations have rendered as "daily" in Matthew and "belonging to the morrow" in Luke. This word has fascinated Hellenic scholars because it appears nowhere else in the Greek language except in the Lord's Prayer. It is possible that this word was created by the early Christian community to describe the Eucharistic meal of fellowship because such a word was needed. The word "Eucharist" had not yet come to be applied and there were no other universally established terms to describe the Christian "breaking of the bread."

When the first Christians prayed the "Our Father" they referred to the entire meal and not just to the elements of bread and wine that we are accustomed to think of in our Eucharistic celebration. The agape (love) feast also consisted of a normal meal of food which preceded the "breaking of bread" (Eucharist). Later — probably beginning with St. Paul in the Corinthian community (1 Cor 11:33, 34a) but more pronounced in the 2nd century — the agape meal was no longer a part of the celebration. There were problems then, as there are today, with respect to "eating together." For example, Paul admonished the Corinthian community (1 Cor 11:20-22) for their lack of fellowship at the meal, and Peter "to his face" and others from Jerusalem who would not "eat" with the Gentile converts (Gal 2:11-14).

The "breaking of bread" as practiced by the early Christians and referred to in the "Our Father" included nourishment for both the body and the soul as well as the fellowship and solidarity of the Christian community. Those not baptized could be a part of the agape meal *preceding* the "breaking of the bread," but had to leave before what we now call the Eucharistic celebration. The basic points to be made here are that the words in the "Our Father" referring to receiving our "daily bread" included the idea of (a) necessary nourishment for both body and soul, (b) the bread of the "morrow" which contained the risen Lord, (c) the celebration of the baptized which included everyone: converted Hellenes, Jews, and persons of every ethnic, racial, economic and social strata who chose to become Christians. The Eucharistic meal was available to them all.

## Lamb of God

St. John the Baptist, in referring to Jesus, said, "Behold the lamb of God" (Jn 1:36). That introductory statement hearkens back in the history of the Jewish people certainly to the time of the Exodus as we have seen.

A lamb is a docile creature. It will stand still while it is being sheared. It will not whimper when it is being led to slaughter. The Jews consumed the lamb to give them strength before they embarked on their journey through the desert seeking the Promised Land. They did not know how long the journey would take or what they would meet along the way.

Today we partake of the Lamb of God in the Eucharist and it sustains us in our daily lives as we journey through the desert of this life.

## Wedding Feast at Cana

The Synoptic Gospels have Jesus beginning His public ministry preceded by John the Baptist as the precursor. In the Gospel of John, Jesus' public ministry begins at the wedding feast at Cana. In this familiar and very touching scene, Jesus' mother, concerned over the possible embarrassment to the wedding couple because they were running out of wine, went to her son and told Him, "They have no wine." His reply was, "Woman, what concern is that to Me? My hour has not yet come." Her response to that was to say to the servers, "Do whatever He tells you" (Jn 2:3-5). Jesus had the six jars used for ceremonial washing filled with water, and asked that some be taken to the chief steward who, after tasting the wine, said to the groom, "Everyone serves the good wine first, and after they have drunk freely an inferior one; but you have kept the best wine until now" (Jn 2:7-10).

The Cana scene is filled with immensely rich instruction and symbolism. The mother of Jesus asks Him to perform His first public miracle with every confidence that He will do so. At first glance it would seem that her concern is only for the bridal couple and the wedding guests. But, in its broader implications, we can discern that the Theotokos (Mother of God) could see the thirst of the world for the precious blood of Jesus. In other words, she is in effect saying, "Son, it is time to begin what You were sent to do. Your people, like the Jews in the desert, are thirsting (for You)."

Jesus, knowing that His time had come, manifests Himself by turning the water into wine. It is, at one and the same time, an epiphany and a prefigurement of the inexhaustible supply of the precious blood of Jesus that will be consecrated on altars throughout the world until the end of time. The beginning of His ministry results in an inexhaustible flow of wine; the end of His ministry will culminate in His giving of the last drop of His precious blood from His wounded side for the salvation of the world (Jn 19:34).

## Miraculous Sharing

There was a miraculous feeding of the Jews in the desert when the Lord God rained down manna in the morning and quail in the evening (Ex 16:4-35). In the Gospels the Lord feeds groups of 5,000 (Mt 14:13-21; Mk 6:34-44; Lk 9:12-17; Jn 6:4-13) and 4,000 (Mk 8:1-9; Mt 15:32-38) with bread and fish provided by others. In John's Gospel the loaves and fish are provided by a young lad (Jn 6:9). An important difference between the Exodus feeding and the feeding of the 5,000 and 4,000 is that in the latter there is a multiplication of a small amount of food which is shared with others. What others contribute is prayed over and distributed so that many can eat. It is a "miraculous sharing." In the Eucharistic celebration, as in the Gospel feedings, the elements that are provided are "the work of human hands."

There is a prefiguring multiplication of loaves account in the Hebrew Scriptures when a man brings 20 loaves to Elisha to feed 100 men and Elisha says, "Give it to the people to eat. For thus says the Lord, 'They shall eat and there shall be some left over'" (2 K 4:42-44). In each of the accounts of the miraculous sharing with the 5,000 and the 4,000 there were leftovers, twelve baskets from the 5,000 and seven baskets from the 4,000.

In the feeding of the 5,000, Matthew reports that Jesus' heart was "moved with pity" (Mt 14:14), and Mark says that "He pitied them" (Mk 6:34). In the feeding of the 4,000 both Matthew (15:23) and Mark (8:2) quote Jesus as saying, "My heart is moved with pity for the crowd." It is out of pity for His hungry brothers and sisters that Jesus feeds His people with the "bread of life." Mark adds, "for they were like sheep without a shepherd" (6:34). Jesus also told the disciples to make the people sit down "on the green grass" (6:39). In Psalm 23, David says, "The Lord is my shepherd, I shall not want. He leads me to lie down in green pastures" (Ps 23:1-2).

Matthew quotes Jesus as saying, "I do not wish to send them away hungry for fear they may collapse on the way" (15:32). Our Lord is with us in our desert journey on the way to the Promised Land of heaven. He pities us and feeds us with His body and blood lest we collapse along the way and give up on our journey to Him.

In the Synoptic Gospels Jesus gives the bread and fish to His disciples to distribute to the people. In the Roman Catholic Church besides the ordinary ministers of the Holy Communion, priests and deacons, lay persons as extraordinary ministers also distribute the Eucharist to the people.

In John's Gospel it is Jesus Who personally distributed the food to the reclining people (6:11). It is probable, however, as in the Synoptic Gospels, that His disciples assisted Him in feeding the 5,000. John, who reports only the feeding of the 5,000, is the sole evangelist who mentions the names of specific disciples in connection with the outdoor banquet. Philip is asked by Jesus, "Where shall we buy bread for these people to eat?" (6:5), and Andrew is quoted as saying, "There is a lad here who has five barley loaves and a couple of dried fish, but what good is that for so many?" (6:9).

In the other accounts of the feedings, those assisting Jesus are only referred to as "disciples" without mentioning specific individuals. The question can then be asked: If the disciples were present at the feeding of the 5,000, why were they so incredulous in the later feeding of the 4,000? Did they not remember the first miraculous sharing? His disciples said to Him, "How could we ever get enough bread in this deserted spot to satisfy such a crowd?" (Mt 15:33); and, "How can anyone give these people sufficient bread in this deserted spot?" (Mk 8:4). Surely they would have remembered the previous feeding of the 5,000.

Whether those present at the second feeding included the Twelve or whether there were other disciples present at the two feedings is not mentioned in either Mark or Matthew. We know that the Twelve were not always present together. They came and they went. What is probable is that there were many more than the Twelve who assisted in the miraculous sharing of both the 5,000 and the 4,000 since it would take considerably more than twelve to distribute the food and pick up the leftovers. These were all referred to as disciples. We know that there were more than twelve disciples appointed for specific work: "The Lord appointed a further seventy (two) others whom He sent ahead of Him in pairs to every town and place He intended to visit" (Lk 10:1).

There were then, in all probability, many disciples who assisted in the miraculous sharing, not just some or all of the Twelve. The Lord calls upon many to distribute the Eucharistic food to His people. The miraculous feedings are a prefigurement of the sharing of the body and blood of Christ.

## The Bread From Heaven

John's Gospel is the only one which does not give an account of the Lord's Supper. The emphasis in this Gospel is on the "bread that came down from heaven" (6:41). In a fascinating discourse between the crowd and Jesus, the crowd claims its ancestral heritage going back to the days when God rained manna on them in the desert and Jesus replies that He is the "real heavenly bread," the "bread of life."

> Your ancestors ate manna in the desert but they died. This is the bread that comes down from heaven for a man to eat and never die. I Myself am the living bread come down from heaven. If anyone eats this bread he shall live forever; the bread I give is My flesh for the life of the world. Let me solemnly assure you, if you

do not eat the flesh of the Son of Man and drink His blood, you have no life in you. He who feeds on My flesh and drinks My blood has life eternal and I will raise him up on the last day. (Jn 6:48-51, 53-54)

The effect of this discourse was that many of Jesus' disciples broke away and would no longer follow Him. This is clearly a teaching by Jesus that He intended to leave us Himself in the form of bread and wine. Many still do not accept the reality of His presence in the Eucharist and consider the bread and wine offered at Mass as merely symbolic. In this clear prefigurement of the Eucharist Jesus challenges our faith to believe that He is truly present in the consecrated bread and wine.

On the road to Emmaus, Jesus, in Luke's Gospel, explained to His fellow travellers all the Scriptures pertaining to Him, beginning with Moses and the prophets. He also celebrated the "breaking of bread" with them. One wonders how much of the above Jesus included in His all-encompassing explanation.

# III

## JEWISH HERITAGE

The prefigurement of the Eucharist in both the Jewish and the Christian Scriptures leads to a brief consideration of how much the early Church and even the modern Church was, and is, indebted to Jewish prayer and customs. Jesus came from a family that followed Jewish devotional and cultic practices. Joseph and Mary were betrothed to one another according to the Jewish practice. On the eighth day after His birth Jesus was circumcised and named according to the Jewish law. If the father is able to perform the circumcision he is not permitted to delegate the function to anyone else (Kolatch, 16).

During the time of Jesus, the circumcision was normally performed by the father in the home. One can imagine that, with the skill that Joseph had with his hands, he performed the circumcision on Jesus. If it wasn't the father, the one who did perform the circumcision and the father were the two primary participants (Ibid., 19).

Again, according to Jewish custom, Jesus, as the first-born male, was presented to the Lord in the Temple on the fortieth day following His birth. At the same time Mary offered herself for purification following the law of Moses, offering in sacrifice "a pair of turtle doves or two young pigeons" (Lk 2:22-24). As devout Jews Joseph and Mary went to Jerusalem every year to celebrate the Passover (Lk 2:41). Jesus came from a devout Jewish family and was a devout Jew.

The early Christians were also devout Jews who met daily in the Temple for prayer and for "breaking bread" (Eucharist) in their homes (Ac 2:46). The first Jewish converts who followed "the way," as it was called, considered themselves Jews who believed in Jesus as the Messiah Who would restore Israel. They continued to attend the synagogue regularly, and it wasn't until 135 CE that the last synagogue door was shut to the Christians.

There was in fact a conflict between the Jews in Jerusalem and the non-Jewish converts in Antioch as to whether the Gentile believers in Jesus as the Messiah needed to follow the Mosaic law with its 613 precepts, including circumcision. It was in Antioch that the name Christian was first applied to the followers of Jesus (Ac 11:26). It was also in Antioch that Paul admonished Peter who at first ate with the Gentile converts but when some people came from James, the head of the Jerusalem church, he separated himself because he was afraid of offending the Jews (Gal 2:11-14). The connotation here goes beyond the mere eating for the nourishment of the body to the Eucharistic celebration which followed.

It was at the first synod of the Church in Jerusalem (46 CE) that James determined that the Gentile converts, which made up the majority of the church of Antioch, did not have to be circumcised but that they should follow the Mosaic law in abstaining from things polluted by idols, from fornication, from whatever has been strangled and from blood (Ac 15:19). While this was a practical compromise it is clear that the Jerusalem church expected that Gentile converts would accept much of the Mosaic law (Ac 15:20). Paul, however, did not limit himself to the synod's concessions and argued forcefully that faith replaced the law entirely (Gal 3:7-29).

While Paul was successful in not imposing the Mosaic law

on the new Christian communities, Jewish prayer, along with cultic and devotional practices were adopted and adapted by them. In the Gospels we find that John the Baptist preached a baptism of repentance, and baptized those who came to him in the Jordan River. During his time converts to Judaism and proselytes were given a *mikva*, a ritual bath enabling an impure person to be restored to a state of purity (Kolatch, 297). In Judaism they were required to be baptized, circumcised and to offer sacrifice. John the Baptist would surely have been familiar with these Jewish practices. Later the Christian community, following Jesus' explicit command (Mt 28:19; Mk 16:16), would baptize their members in the name of the Holy Trinity (Father, Son, and Holy Spirit) in a ritual not unlike that of the *mikva*.

The three centers of Jewish worship during the time of Jesus and the beginning of Christianity were the Temple, the synagogue and the home.

The Temple was the site for Israel's sacrificial cultic worship. It was also a place for individual personal prayer since it was considered a special place of God's presence. Here the sacrifice of animals took place. The Temple was also a place where the wise and learned would teach. Jesus and His disciples followed this tradition and often taught there.

It was David's idea to build a Temple to house the ark of the covenant but it was Solomon who built the first Temple. It was a part of the palace enclosure and the king had his own gate from the palace to the Temple court. The palace was a much more extensive structure than the Temple. The Temple of Solomon was destroyed by the Babylonians in 587 BCE.

The Temple of Zerubbabel, the second Temple, after some delays in construction, was dedicated in 515 BCE. It stood until the beginning of the construction of Herod's Temple in 19 BCE. Herod, who was not a Jew, built the Temple to appease the Jews. The building was an extensive structure which was built in ten years but not completely finished until 64 CE, six years before it was destroyed by the Romans in their attack on Jerusalem in 70 CE.

There has been no effort to build a Temple since then. The Christian priesthood is prefigured by the Jewish priesthood which served the Temple. During Jesus' time there was the High Priest and eight to ten other priests connected with the Temple. The bulk of the priesthood served at the Temple twice a year for a period of four weeks each, once for holy days and the other during what we would call ordinary time. While serving at the Temple they abstained from sexual relations with their wives. When not serving in the Temple the Jewish priests would return to their secular lives as farmers, merchants, etc. While there is no direct proof, this abstention could very well have contributed to priestly celibacy in Christian Churches. For the Christian, the Temple sacrifice is a prefigurement of the Eucharist which replaced the animal sacrifices of the Temple with the ultimate sacrifice offered by Jesus of Himself to God.

The second center of Jewish worship was, and continues to be, the synagogue. Any ten men can establish a synagogue and there is no particular structure needed with worship taking place in a suitable locale. A priest attending a synagogue had no greater role than other participants. The priest's role and functions were connected with the Temple. When Herod's Temple was destroyed the priesthood ceased to exist.

The synagogue was probably established as a result of the destruction of the Temple in 587 BCE and the dispersion of the Jews to Babylon. By Jesus' time the synagogue was an essential part of Jewish life. It had a distinct building and was found in every Palestinian town even in the small village of Nazareth at which the holy family participated. It was also established by Jews living abroad and was the major means of continuing Jewish life and cult. It is in the synagogue that the Scriptures are read and discussed during a service of the Word. Jesus and His disciples used it as a place of prayer and evangelization (Lk 4:16-21; Ac 13:15-16). The Christian Church adopted this service of the Word and added the Christian sacraments. When a local church had to separate from the synagogue it still followed the synagogue pattern of worship as we can see in Paul's ministry from the Acts of the Apostles:

> He entered the synagogue and for three months spoke out boldly, and argued persuasively about the kingdom of God. When some stubbornly refused to believe and spoke evil of the Way before the congregation, he left them, taking the disciples with him, and argued daily in the lecture hall of Tyrannus. This continued for two years, so that all the residents of Asia, both Jews and Greeks, heard the word of the Lord (19:8-10).

The synagogue Sabbath service served as a model for what later became the Liturgy of the Word in the Christian Mass. Both Jewish and Christian services include readings from Scripture, periods of prayer, and acclamations. The central acclamation in the synagogue service was, and is, "Amen," which Christians adopted untranslated.

The Jewish practices of praying during the day, a respect for the time of day, a sanctification of the day, have also been adopted by Christianity. The Jewish method of determining time is used in the liturgical practice of the Christian Church. The day is considered to be from dusk to dusk. The Jewish Sabbath begins on Friday evening at dusk, and the Christian Sunday begins with Evening Prayer (Vespers) on Saturday evening.

The Jewish tradition is to pray three times a day, morning, midday, and evening. Every Jew would pray three times a day whether they were at home, traveling, or at the synagogue. Christians adopted the Jewish practice of praying three times at morning, midday, and evening. The *Didache* required that the Lord's Prayer be prayed three times a day. A modern Catholic prayer practice is to pray the Angelus at 6:00 a.m., at noon, and once again at 6:00 p.m.

The real center for Jewish worship can be said to be the home. Like the synagogue it is lay-centered around prayer and Scripture. Parents have the duty of instructing their children in the Scriptures, explaining them, discussing them, and praying with their children. It is said that a mother would put a drop of honey on the Scriptures and have her child kiss the Scriptures so that he or she would gain a love of the word of God.

The family meal is also a strong form of Jewish worship and piety. Sabbath meals are family liturgical celebrations, full of joy, with special prayers to remember God's goodness. The emphasis on Scripture and prayer both in the synagogue and at home and the sacredness of the meal serve to keep the covenant of the Lord in mind at all times. The sacredness of the meal and, in particular, the Passover meal, gave meaning to the "breaking of bread" by Jews who believed that Jesus was the Messiah. The Passover feast is a feast of liturgical remembering and Jesus at the Last Supper said, "Do this in memory (remembrance) of Me" (Lk 22:19; 1 Cor 11:24, 25).

The sharing of a Jewish meal as a sacred act results in the praise of God for the gifts given. The "barekh" is a Jewish prayer that begins and/or ends by blessing God: "Blessed are you, our God...." It is a prayer of thanksgiving and praise. At the Last Supper Jesus is described as blessing the bread before breaking it (Mk 14:22; Mt 26:26; Lk 22:19). The shape or form of the "barekh" prayer would seem to have influenced the Eucharistic prayer.

The structure of the Jewish sacred meal has also contributed to the form of the Christian Eucharist. For example, the master of the house, or at his request, the most distinguished guest, would invite everyone to prayer. He would take the cup of benediction (Kos shell barekh), lift it up, and with his eyes on it pronounce the prescribed blessings. All would reply, "Amen." Then they would drink from the cup. In Luke, Jesus "took a cup, gave thanks, and said, 'Take this and share it among yourselves...'" (22:17). Only in Luke is the first cup mentioned.

In the modern Passover meal the first cup of wine, "Kiddush: the blessing of wine," is lifted up and the blessing is recited with the leader saying, "Blessed are you, Lord our God, ruler of the universe, creator of the fruit of the vine." To which the participants add, "Praised are you, Lord our God, ruler of the universe, who has chosen us among all peoples and sanctified us with your commandments. With an everlasting love you have given us holidays and seasons for rejoicing and this day of the Feast of the Matzo, the time of our freedom, in remembrance of Israel's going out from Egypt. Blessed are you, Lord our God, who sanctifies Israel and the festival seasons."

All drink of the first cup of wine.

There are four cups of wine offered and consumed in a Passover or Seder meal. The second cup is "The Cup of Memory," reminding those present that God not only freed the Jews from slavery in Egypt, but is a reminder of each generation's need for salvation. In 1 Corinthians 11:25 there is a call for remembrance in offering the cup: "Do this, as often as you drink it, in remembrance of Me." The third cup offered is "The Cup of Redemption," celebrating God's promise of redemption. The fourth cup is "The Cup of Hope and Freedom," a reminder of freedom, its hopes, struggles and dreams for all nations and all peoples.

The Christian "breaking of bread" is also influenced by the Jewish custom at meals. The head of the table, before distributing the bread, pronounces a blessing, "Barekh." In the Passover meal there is also the blessing over the unleavened bread, the Matzo, the eating of the bitter herb, the eating of the bitter herb along with the Matzo, the eating of the Passover meal, the Barekh or grace after the meal, the recital of Psalms, followed by the fourth cup, as above, and the final benediction.

We do not know exactly how the Passover meal was celebrated in Jesus' time since there have inevitably been changes over the years but the same basic pattern and spirit has prevailed.

It is clear that Judaism has contributed much to Christianity in its manner of worship, prayer, respect for and use of Sacred Scripture, forms of blessing (Barekh), the structure of the liturgy and the sacredness of the ritual meal.

# IV

## GREEK HERITAGE

There is a dearth of understanding in the West with regard to its Eastern heritage. Pope John Paul II said, "Since we believe that the venerable and ancient tradition of the Eastern Churches is an integral part of the heritage of Christ's Church, the first need of Catholics is to be familiar with that tradition so as to be nourished by it and to encourage the process of unity in the best way possible for each" (*The Light of the East*, 1). He further states, "Contact with this glorious tradition is most fruitful for the Church. As the Council points out: 'From their very origins the Churches of the East have had a treasury from which the Church of the West has amply drawn for its liturgy, spiritual tradition and jurisprudence" (*Ut Unum Sint*, 57).

The first six ecumenical councils of the Christian Church established the basic theology and settled the fundamental questions regarding Christology, Mariology, and Trinitarian theology. These councils were largely attended by Greek bishops from Eastern Christianity who debated these issues and established basic dogma. There was a minimum participation by Western bishops in these ecumenical councils. At the first ecumenical council, Nicea I (325), 220 bishops participated but only a handful were from the West. Greek speaking bishops made up all of the bishops participating at Constantinople I (381), and most of those at Ephesus (431), Chalcedon (451), Constantinople II (553), and Constantinople III (680-81). Nicea II (787) largely dealt with the problem of iconoclasm. Only these first seven councils are mutually recognized by the Roman Catholic and Orthodox Churches. The Orthodox Churches regard them as the only councils which can be called ecumenical.

Vatican II in its *Decree on Ecumenism* had this to say on the contribution of the East to the Church of the West:

> From their very origins the Churches of the East have had a treasury from which the Church of the West has drawn largely for its liturgy, spiritual tradition and jurisprudence. Nor must we underestimate the fact that the basic dogmas of the Christian faith concerning the Trinity and the word of God made flesh from the Virgin Mary were defined in Ecumenical Councils held in the East. (III, I, 14)

The fundamental question facing the first six councils was, "Who is Jesus?"

Our understanding of what we receive in Holy Communion today is shaped by what these six councils defined with regard to Jesus' humanity and divinity, His relationship to the Father, and Mary's relationship to Jesus as God and human being.

The Roman emperor Constantine allowed Christians to worship with the edict of Milan in 313. Twelve years later, because of the division within Christianity caused by Arius, Constantine called a council of the Church's bishops (Nicea I, 325). Arius taught that Jesus was not eternal and uncreated like God the Father. Constantine exerted strong leadership over the proceedings, calling the council, holding the meetings in his palace in present day Turkey, presiding at the beginning, addressing the members and confirming and promulgating its decrees.

Pope Sylvester did not attend but sent two delegates in his name. Some 220 to 250 bishops participated with only the two papal delegates from the West. Athanasius, Bishop Alexander of Alexandria's deacon, led the effort that produced a statement which declared Jesus' equality with His Father. The council used the word "homoousios" to define the fact that Jesus is "one in being" or "of the same being" or "of the same substance" as the Father.

Nicea I, which produced the Nicene Creed, did not stop the Arian heresy for the Arians continued to teach that Jesus was not fully divine. It was the Greek Cappadocians, Basil of Caesarea, Gregory of Nazianzus and Gregory of Nyssa who further developed the relationship of the Holy Spirit to the Father and the Son. Basil in his treatise *On the Holy Spirit*, stressed that the Holy Spirit together with the Father and the Son is to be worshiped and glorified. Nicea had merely stated, "We believe in the Holy Spirit" (Denzinger-Schönmetzer, *Enchiridion Symbolorum*, 125). Basil, however, refrained from explicitly calling the Holy Spirit, "God." It was Basil's friend and fellow bishop, Gregory of Nazianzus, who first indicated that the Holy Spirit cannot be other than God, proceeding from the Father's bounty. Basil's brother, Gregory of Nyssa gave theological language to the relationship of the Father, Son and Holy Spirit. They were one in being or substance (ousia), but three in subsistence (hypostasis, or persona in Latin).

The Emperor Theodosius, who made Christianity the only legal religion in the Roman Empire, called another council, Constantinople I, in 381. This council gave formal recognition to the Cappadocian Fathers' work, reaffirmed the Nicene Creed and defined the relationship of the Holy Spirit to the Father and the Son declaring, "the Spirit, the holy, the lordly and life-giving one, proceeding forth from the Father, co-worshiped and co-glorified with the Father and the Son" (Bellitto, 21).

John Zizioulas explains the Greek Fathers' early view with respect to the invocation of the Holy Spirit:

> In the celebration of the Eucharist, the Church very early realized that in order for the Eucharistic community to become or reveal in itself the wholeness of the Body of Christ (a wholeness that would include not only humanity but the entire creation), the descent of the Holy Spirit upon this creation would be necessary. The offering up of the gifts and the whole community to the throne of God, the realization of the unity of the Body of Christ, was therefore preceded by the *invocation of the Holy Spirit*. "Send down thy Holy Spirit upon *us* and upon the *gifts* placed before thee" (Liturgy of St. John Chrysostom). For the world to become even symbolically a real sign of the consummation of all in Christ would be an impossibility without the Holy Spirit. The Eucharistic community shows by its very existence that the realization of the Church's catholicity in history is the work of the Holy Spirit. (*Being as Communion*, 160)

The liturgy of St. Basil makes it clear that the Holy Spirit is invoked not just for the consecration of the gifts but also for the realization of the unity of the community: "to unite us all, as many as are partakers in the one bread and cup, one with another, in the communion of the one Holy Spirit" (Ibid.).

From a Eucharistic focus we can see that it is the Holy Spirit that gives life to the offered bread and wine and that what is consumed is Jesus, Who is one in being with the Father. It is the Holy Spirit that formed Jesus in Mary's womb (Lk 1:35; Mt 1:20). It is that same Spirit that transforms the bread and wine into the body and blood of Jesus. It is the same Holy Spirit that unites the community, for all partake of the same loaf.

Pope Damasus I did not send any delegates to Constantinople I, but the West as well as the East consider this council as ecumenical.

The problems connected with "Who is Jesus?" continued. How was Jesus one person, both human and divine? Was He really two separate natures and at the same time one merged person? These questions also have a Eucharistic relationship. What are we receiving when we receive Holy Communion? With respect to Jesus' mother, was she the mother of the human Jesus only? Nestorius, bishop of Constantinople, who was against Arianism, taught that Mary was the mother of the human Jesus but not the mother of God. This meant that Jesus was two separate persons. Cyril of Alexandria, a follower of Athanasius, opposed Nestorius.

Emperor Theodosius II called the third ecumenical council at Ephesus in 431. The eastern bishops condemned Nestorius, recognized Mary as the Theotokos (she who brings God forth), and said that Jesus had a human and divine nature united in one person.

Since the Theotokos is the mother of God who gave Him flesh, she is also the "mother of the Eucharist."

Despite the work of the first three ecumenical councils — Nicea, Constantinople I and Ephesus — there was still confusion by some as to Who Jesus was. More precise language was needed. For example, some taught that Jesus' divine nature overwhelmed and canceled out his human nature. That Jesus had one nature, divine, was known as Monophysitism. If this were true then the Eucharist would contain only the God Jesus, and not His human nature as well.

Marcian, Theodosius' successor, called a council meeting at Chalcedon in 451. The most important doctrinal declaration that came from this council was that Jesus is one person with two natures joined together in a hypostatic union. The two natures were separate but equal. The divine nature did not overcome Jesus' human nature: "...our Lord Jesus Christ: the same truly God and truly man, of a rational soul and a body; co-substantial with the Father as regards His divinity, and the same co-substantial with us as regards His humanity; like us in all respects except for sin..." (Bellitto, 26). While only half a dozen bishops attended from the West, Pope Leo's *Tome* on the nature of Jesus was acclaimed and included in the Chalcedon documents. Pope Gregory I (590-604) said that these first four ecumenical councils were as authoritative as the four Gospels (Ibid., 27).

The early councils were not called by the popes or the patriarchs but by the emperors. There was jockeying and political intrigue by the supporters of various views on the nature of Jesus. For the sake of peace, the emperor was urged to take a particular stand or to call a council meeting. Despite the development of precise theological language on the nature and personhood of Jesus by the first four councils, those who supported Nestorianism and Monophysitism continued their efforts.

In 553 Emperor Justinian called another ecumenical council. The Empress Theodora, a powerful person, favored Monophysitism and had helped get Vigilius elected pope with the understanding that he would support the idea that Jesus' divine nature overpowered His human nature. Vigilius wrote to Justinian several times indicating that he would support Chalcedon. Although he was in Constantinople Vigilius did not attend the council. Theodora died in 548 making it easier for Justinian to move against the Nestorians and Monophysites. Justinian led Constantinople II without Vigilius. When the council condemned the writings of those opposed to Chalcedon, Vigilius at first refused to comply. When Justinian produced Vigilius' letters supporting Chalcedon he relented and agreed with the condemnations.

Constantinople II (553) strongly condemned heretical documents on the nature of Jesus and issued fourteen anathemas against them. The council again clarified the teaching that Jesus' two natures were united hypostatically in His one person and supported Nicea I, Constantinople I, Ephesus and Chalcedon strengthening the teachings of these first four ecumenical councils in developing early Church dogma on the nature and person of Jesus.

While the first five ecumenical councils precisely developed the dogma on the nature and person of Jesus, there arose another problem: the will of Jesus. Since Jesus was one person with two natures, did He have one will or two wills? Monothelitism taught that Jesus' human will was merged with His divine will. In response to this Pope Agatho called for local synods and a Roman synod to consider this matter. Agatho and Emperor Constantine IV decided that it was necessary to call another ecumenical council, Constantinople III (680-81), to consider this matter.

Like most early councils it was comprised primarily of Eastern bishops; however, because of the early work of the synods, the West contributed significantly to this council. Monothelitism was condemned and the council declared that the one person Jesus has two wills, one human and one divine, which coincided with His human and divine natures.

The first six ecumenical councils developed the basic Christology, Mariology and Trinitarian theology for the Church. The bishops attending these councils were overwhelmingly from the East of Hellenic heritage. We owe much to them for laying the foundation of Church dogma. Who Jesus is, brought forth by the Theotokos as true God and true man, and His relationship to the Father and the Holy Spirit, all have a direct influence on Eucharistic theology.

Much more can be said of the contribution of the early Eastern Fathers to our understanding of the Eucharist, not the least of which was that in the West the Eucharistic language was Greek until sometime around the third century when it was changed to Latin. The early Greek Father, St. Ignatius of Antioch (about 35-107), in his letters to the various churches on his way to martyrdom in Rome, taught that the life of Christ is continued for all time in the Eucharist, which he calls "the bread that is the flesh of Christ...." He called Holy Communion "a medicine of immortality and an antidote of death" (*Ephesians,* 20). Ignatius emphasized that the Church must gather around the bishop for the celebration of the Eucharist. Other early Greek Fathers who made important contributions to the doctrinal beliefs regarding the Eucharist include: St. John Chrysostom (347-407), St. Cyril of Jerusalem (315-386), St. Gregory of Nyssa (330-395) and St. Cyril of Alexandria (d. 444).

St. Cyril of Alexandria, as noted above, was the great protagonist against the Nestorian heresy at Ephesus. He had great devotion to the Holy Eucharist and emphasized the effects it has on those who receive it worthily. He said that by Holy Communion we are made con-corporeal with Christ. He affirmed with conviction and vigor his Eucharistic doctrine. In a letter to Nestorius, which received the assent of the bishops at Ephesus, he wrote:

> Proclaiming the death according to the flesh of the only begotten Son of God, that is Jesus Christ, and confessing his resurrection from the dead and ascent into heaven, we celebrate the bloodless sacrifice in our churches; and thus approach the mystic blessings, and are sanctified by partaking of the holy flesh and the precious blood of Christ the savior of us all. And we receive it, not as common flesh (God forbid), nor as the flesh of a man sanctified and associated with the Word according to the unity of merit, or as having a

divine indwelling, but as really the life-giving and very flesh of the Word himself. (Migne, PG, lxxvii, 113, Butler, Vol. I, 285)

And in a letter to Calosyrius, Bishop of Arsinoe:

I hear that they say that the sacramental consecration does not avail for hallowing a portion of it to be kept to another day. In saying this they are crazy. For Christ is not altered, nor will his holy body be changed; but the power of the consecration and the life-giving grace still remain in it. (Migne, PG, lxxvi, 1073, Ibid.)

St. John Chrysostom, Archbishop of Constantinople (347-407), known as "the golden mouth" because of the sweetness and fluency of his eloquence, spoke with great tenderness on the divine love which is displayed in the Holy Eucharist and exhorted the faithful to frequent Holy Communion.

The Western Church considers him along with St. Basil (329-379), St. Gregory of Nazianzus (329-390), and St. Athanasius (295-373) as the four great Greek doctors. St. Pius X, in 1909, declared St. John Chrysostom as the heavenly patron of preachers of the Word of God. The four are among the early Greek Fathers who helped develop devotion to and understanding of the infinite value of the Holy Eucharist.

# V

## THE LORD'S SUPPER

The climax of Jesus' public ministry takes place at the Last Supper which He had with His disciples. He knew that He was about to leave the earth and His love was so great that He desired to leave His corporeal presence with His followers to sustain them on their journey. Human beings are flesh and blood and need a tangible presence to remind them. "Do this in memory of Me" (Lk 22:19). Human flesh and blood is fed with the flesh and blood of eternity.

It was at a Jewish meal that Jesus initiated the holy Sacrament of Himself. He said, "I have eagerly desired to eat this Passover with you before I suffer" (Lk 22:15). He sent two of His disciples to make preparations for the meal. In Luke they are identified as Peter and John (22:8). On this, the most solemn Jewish feast day, all devout Jews had, if possible, to celebrate in Jerusalem. The population of the city exploded and the residents were required to provide hospitality. The master of the house welcomed the two disciples and showed them a large furnished upper room where they prepared the Passover. During Passover no charge was permitted for providing housing or a place to celebrate the feast.

Joachim Jeremias estimates that to a resident Jerusalem population of 25-30,000 were added some 85 to 125,000 pilgrims. Others have estimated that at times the total number in Jerusalem swelled up to a million persons. The Jewish historian Flavius Josephus and the Roman historian Tacitus estimated that "not less than three million" celebrated Passover in Jerusalem in the year 65 CE (Kolatch, 185). While this was some 32 years after Jesus' celebration of the Lord's Supper it would appear that Jeremias' estimate of 85 to 125,000 pilgrims for that year's celebration is probably low.

The majority of the pilgrims had to sleep in tents which were set up all around Jerusalem, particularly on the plain to the north of the city. We must remember that the Jews were once a nomadic people and living in tents brought back memories of the past. Before 621 BCE the Passover had been a domestic festival; after that year it became a cultic feast.

It became impossible to eat the Passover sacrifice in the Temple fore-courts. From the first century BCE only the slaughter of animals took place in the Temple area. From then on the Passover meal was transferred to the houses of Jerusalem. It was also not possible for all the pilgrims to spend the Passover night in Jerusalem as was called for by Deuteronomy 16:7. Permission was given for the Passover night (not the Passover meal) to be spent in the environs of Jerusalem. That is why, it is conjectured, that Jesus left the holy city in the evening during His last stay in Jerusalem (Mk 11:11, 19; 14:3; Lk 21:37; 22:39). He remained in the overcrowded city for the Last Supper because the Passover meal had to be eaten within the gates of Jerusalem. Despite the coldness of the season many were forced to eat the Passover in courtyards and on rooftops (Jeremias 42, 43). The Passover includes a period of seven days with the paschal lamb eaten on the first day; only unleavened bread was to be eaten during the period of the feast (Dt 16:3, 4, 8).

The Passover meal celebrated by Jesus stands out as a special one among the meals He participated in during His ministry. As the first-born male Jesus was required on the day before the Passover to fast. This requirement is based on the sparing of the first-born Jewish males while the Egyptian first-born males were slain (Ex 12:21-28; Kolatch, 186). Jeremias believes that Jesus fasted and did not partake of the bread or the wine He offered at the Last Supper.

## 1 Corinthians

If we review the writings on what Jesus said in offering His body and blood at the Last Supper chronologically, we would have to start with Paul's recitation in 1 Corinthians, which was written about the year 56 CE:

> For I received from the Lord what I also handed on to you, that the Lord Jesus, on the night He was handed over, took bread, and after He had given thanks, broke it and said, "This is My body that is for you. Do this in remembrance of Me." In the same way also the cup, after supper, saying, "This cup is the new covenant in My blood. Do this as often as you drink it, in remembrance of Me." For as often as you eat this bread and drink the cup, you proclaim the death of the Lord until He comes. Therefore whoever eats the bread or drinks the cup of the Lord unworthily will have to answer for the body and blood of the Lord. A person should examine himself, and so eat the bread and drink the cup. For anyone who eats and drinks without discerning the body, eats and drinks judgment on himself. (1 Cor 11:23-29)

Paul had more problems with the irascible Corinthian community than with any of the other Christian communities he established. During Paul's time it had only some 40-50 members (J. Murphy-O'Connor, meeting). Within that community were those whose moral values allowed them to sleep with whomever they pleased, approved of incest, men and women who attired themselves in such a way that obscured their sexual differences, and some who denied the resurrection. In addition to the two letters he wrote to the Corinthians, he sent Timothy and Titus at different times to Corinth to mediate and represent him. Later, Clement of Rome also sent a letter to the Corinthians reminding them of Paul's teachings. Paul, however, never gave up on this fledgling church and called them his "beloved children."

Before reviewing with them the words of institution above, Paul admonished them for not being a united community which cared for one another when they met to have their agape supper meal before celebrating the Lord's Supper. The rich huddled together, ate and got drunk while the poor went hungry.

Without unity, without the proper Christ-like attitude, then it is not the Lord's Supper that they eat (11:20). Anyone who receives the bread and drinks the cup unworthily will have to answer for this. Anyone who does not discern the body perpetuates division and brings "judgment on himself" (11:29).

With regard to the words of institution, Paul is the only one who uses "in remembrance of Me" in offering both the body and the cup. Paul's version of these words is closest to Luke who traveled with Paul. Luke uses "in memory of Me" only in offering the bread. Both indicate that it is for their sake ("given for you") in offering the body. Both refer to the cup as "the new covenant of My blood." Both mention the offering of the cup after the supper. Neither Mark nor Matthew have these traits in their accounts of the Last Supper.

Paul teaches us the necessity for Eucharistic discernment and unity.

## Mark's Gospel

Mark's Gospel was probably written some time between 65 CE and 70 CE. Some believe it could have extended to the early 70's. It is the earliest of the Gospels. Mark traveled with Paul and Barnabas on their first missionary journey. Because Mark had left to go home during this journey, Paul insisted that Mark not accompany them on the second journey. Barnabas, Mark's uncle, and Paul differed and Barnabas left for Cyprus with Mark, and Paul took off with Silas on his second missionary journey (Ac 15:39, 40).

There is question as to whether this is the same Mark who wrote the Gospel. Nowhere does the author identify himself. The heading "according to Mark" was not a part of the original text but added later. Mark was a common name. If it is the same Mark who participated in the first missionary journey then he was apparently reconciled with Paul and rejoined him (2 Tm 4:1; Phm 24; Col 4:10). There are also three mentions of "John Mark" in the Acts of the Apostles (12:12, 12:25, 15:37-39).

Mark is also mentioned in 1 Peter (5:13): "Your sister church in Babylon sends you greetings and so does my son Mark." Babylon was a code name for Rome. Early tradition indicates that Mark acted as Peter's interpreter and wrote the Gospel from Peter's story.

Both Luke and Matthew had Mark's Gospel in hand and appropriated much of it in their respective Gospels. Some 80% of Mark's verses are reproduced in Matthew's Gospel and 65% in Luke's. Mark's Gospel is written for a community that is either about to or is undergoing persecution. The emphasis in Mark's Gospel is the cross. Many commentators believe the tradition that the setting for the composition of the Gospel is Rome after the martyrdom of Peter and Paul during the persecution that followed the great fire of 64 CE, under Nero. Some believe it was written in Galilee, or near Palestine. Since the early missionaries were peripatetic it could have been started in one place and finished in another, with insertions along the way. The words of institution of the Holy Eucharist in Mark are as follows:

> While they were eating, He took bread, said the blessing, broke it and gave it to them and said, "Take it; this is My body." Then He took the cup, gave thanks, and gave it to them, and they all drank from it. He said to them, "This is My blood of the covenant which will be shed for many. Amen I say to you, I shall not drink again the fruit of the vine until the day when I drink it anew in the kingdom of God." (14:22-25)

The majority of scholars believe that the Markan and Matthean Last Supper verses reflect a Jerusalem tradition while Luke and Paul reflect an Antiochene tradition. If the author, Mark, is the one associated with Peter, the words of institution could very well have had a Petrine influence.

When the meal was held and what kind of meal was consumed is in continuous dispute. The Synoptics and Paul place the meal on the eve of Passover while John places it on the day of preparation when the Paschal lambs were slain. It could be that each was following a different calendar and there may have been variations in celebrating the Passover during Jesus' time. Jeremias concludes that Jesus fasted during the meal and did not partake of the offering of the bread and the wine as His body and blood. We saw earlier that it was Jewish tradition that the first born male fasted on the day before Passover which would give credibility to the Johannine approach.

The Feast of Unleavened Bread and Passover were two distinct celebrations which by the time of Jesus were celebrated together. The Feast of Unleavened Bread was a yearly agricultural feast which thanked God for the annual spring harvest by offering without yeast or leaven the first wheat harvested. It also professed that all the harvest belonged to God and was given to human beings for their nourishment. Since they both occurred in the Spring the two feasts were eventually celebrated together.

Unleavened bread was eaten by the Israelites at their sudden departure from Egypt because there was no time to make bread from yeast. Mark's Gospel was referring to the Feast of Unleavened Bread when Jesus sent His disciples to prepare the supper: "On the day of the Feast of Unleavened Bread, when they sacrificed the Passover lamb, His disciples said to Him, 'Where do You want us to go and prepare for You to eat the Passover?'" (14:12). This would be the Day of Preparation on Wednesday, when the lambs were sacrificed in the Temple. However, since the days were calculated as beginning after sundown (6:00 p.m.), the meal was probably eaten on early Thursday, the beginning of the new day, but in the evening. Since the day would go for twenty-four hours, by our reckoning of time, Jesus was crucified on Friday, but still within the twenty-four hours of Thursday by the reckoning of Jewish time. The differences in our reckoning of time, at which the new day begins at midnight, has contributed to the confusion of when Jesus celebrated the Last Supper.

While there is no mention of consuming lamb, Mark's account still suggests a Passover supper. However, the account uses the Greek word *artos* as the bread offered, which is leavened bread rather than *azyma* which is unleavened bread. This is one of the reasons given by the Orthodox Church that it was not a Passover meal.

Mark's words of institution emphasize that the bread and wine truly bear the presence of Jesus and inaugurate a new covenant which will be fully realized in the kingdom of God. The Markan emphasis is on the complete self-giving by Jesus which is to be culminated on the cross.

## Matthew's Gospel

Matthew's Gospel was written sometime around 80-85 CE. It was written for a largely Jewish Christian community that still considered itself Jewish and worshiped in the synagogue. After the destruction of the Temple in 70 CE this Jewish Christian community competed with other Jewish groups, particularly with the early rabbinic movement, consisting primarily of scribes and Pharisees. Matthew tried to show that the Jewish tradition could best be preserved in a Jewish-Christian context.

Matthew presents Jesus as the authoritative interpreter of the Torah, as opposed to the authority of the scribes and Pharisees as the interpreters of this, the most basic of Jewish Scriptures. The original text did not name the author and the title "according to Matthew" was not part of the first edition. Nowhere in the text does the author claim to have been an eyewitness to what he describes. There is a preponderant agreement among scholars that the author is not the tax collector (9:9) who became an apostle. He is an anonymous author.

Raymond Brown, the distinguished biblical scholar, has concluded that none of the Gospels were written by an eyewitness to the events. As indicated above, Matthew appropriates some eighty percent of the verses in Mark. In addition to Mark, his sources include what scholars refer to as "Q" (from the German word quelle), information available to both Matthew and Luke, and his own contribution referred to as "M." Q has not been found as a separate document but is deduced from the Gospels of Matthew and Luke. Almost all commentators locate the composition of Matthew's Gospel in Palestine or Syria.

While Matthew relies heavily on Mark he freely edits Mark and joins it to Q and material peculiar to Matthew. Matthew added to the Markan narratives large blocks of theological teaching by Jesus. As a largely Jewish community the law and its observance were more important issues for the Matthean compared to the Markan community. For the same reason it was more important for Matthew to root Jesus in the Jewish Scriptures.

The words of institution in Matthew's Last Supper account are:

> While they were eating Jesus took bread, said the blessing, broke it and giving it to His disciples said, "Take and eat; this is My body." Then He took the cup, gave thanks, and gave it to them saying, "Drink from it, all of you, for this is My blood of the covenant, which will be shed on behalf of many for the forgiveness of sins. I tell you, from now on I shall not drink this fruit of the vine until the day when I drink it with you anew in the kingdom of My Father." (26:26-29)

Jesus begins with a blessing that would have been common at Jewish Sabbath and holiday meals. His blessing is not so much a consecration as it is a thanksgiving. The successive actions of taking bread, giving thanks, of pronouncing a blessing (addressed to God, not the bread), breaking and distributing, are common for the Jewish grace during a meal as Jesus did during the feeding of the five thousand (14:19) and the four thousand (15:36).

"Take and eat; this is My body" gives new meaning to what is customary at Jewish meals, viz., sharing the loaf of bread and the cup of wine. Sharing in Jesus' bread, i.e., His body, means sharing in His death.

Matthew adds the imperative "eat" to Mark's version. As in Mark there is no interval of supper (as in 1 Cor 11:25; Lk 22:20) when Jesus offers the cup: "Drink from it, all of you...." Unlike Mark ("and all drank from it") this is expressed as a command from Jesus.

"This is My blood of the covenant" refers to Exodus 24:8

where Moses seals God's covenant with Israel by sprinkling the people with animal blood.

"Shed for many" alludes to Isaiah 53:12 ("And he shall take away the sins of many"). "Many" does not refer to some as opposed to all, but in the Semitic usage, to the whole of humankind as opposed to the one making the sacrifice.

"…for the forgiveness of sins," is a distinct contribution by Matthew to the Last Supper accounts. In his description of John the Baptist's baptism, Matthew specifically avoids calling it a baptism for "the remission of sins" (see Mt 3:11 as opposed to Mk 1:4). The very words in Mark which have John the Baptist proclaiming a baptism of repentance "for the forgiveness of sins" are utilized by Matthew in his Eucharistic prayer.

"From now on I will not drink this fruit of the vine until I drink it with you anew in the kingdom of My Father." Jesus' Last Supper anticipates the banquet in God's kingdom. It is in "the kingdom of My Father." In Matthew there are more than twenty mentions of "Father" for God, against two in Mark and ten in Luke. Only the Gospel of John has more occurrences than Matthew, but in John it is almost primarily as the Father of Jesus.

Matthew adds the words "from now on" which alludes to Jesus' forthcoming passion, and the words "and with you" which emphasizes His relationship with His disciples and anticipates their joining Him in the fulfillment of the kingdom and stresses Jesus' union with His Church through the Eucharist.

The changes in Matthew in comparison to Mark's version of the words of institution probably reflect the Matthean experience of liturgy in his community. The words of consecration are a self-contained unit which would fit neatly into a larger Eucharistic prayer.

## Luke's Gospel

Luke's Gospel was written at about the same time as Matthew's Gospel, around 80-90 CE. He is also the author of the Acts of the Apostles. Tradition identifies the author as a Syrian from Antioch who is mentioned in Colossians 4:14, Philemon 24, and Timothy 4:11. He wrote in high-class Greek and was versed in both the Jewish Scriptures and Hellenistic writings. Luke indicates in the prologue of the Gospel that he is not an eyewitness to the events but is dependent upon traditions he has received from those who were eyewitnesses and ministers of the Word. His sources include the Gospel of Mark from which he appropriated some sixty-five percent of the verses, "Q" as explained above, and a tradition peculiar to Luke. He was writing to an audience largely made up of Gentile Christians. The Lukan words of consecration are as follows:

> When the hour came, He took His place at table with the apostles. He said to them, "I have eagerly desired to eat this Passover with you before I suffer, for, I tell you I shall not eat it [again] until there is fulfillment in the kingdom of God." Then He took a cup, gave thanks, and said, "Take this and share it among yourselves; for I tell you [that] from this time on I shall not drink of the fruit of the vine until the kingdom of God comes." Then He took the bread, said the blessing, broke it, and gave it to them, saying, "This is My body, which will be given for you; do this in memory of Me." And likewise the cup after they had eaten, saying, "This cup is the new covenant in My blood, which shall be shed for you." (Lk 22:14-20)

Luke's introduction differs from those in Mark (14:18-21) and Matthew (26:21-25). Jesus begins with "I have eagerly desired to eat this Passover with you before I suffer" (22:15). This is unique to Luke and indicates the importance of this meal to Jesus' followers. Mark and Matthew begin with the prediction of the betrayal. Luke leaves this until after the offering of the bread and wine. And when Jesus says that He "will not eat it [again] until there is fulfillment in the kingdom of God" He could be talking about the Second Coming but most probably is referring to the institution of the kingdom after His resurrection.

Everything then is in place. Jesus fulfills His mission by His incarnation, His passion and His resurrection. The kingdom is established, the victory has been won. It is only a question of time. What may seem to be an interminably long time for the Second Coming by those who are subject to time is insignificant from a heavenly perspective. The kingdom is in place. The complete fulfillment of the kingdom is inevitable.

In Luke's account the cup is offered twice while Mark and Matthew have only one offering of the cup, after the offering of the bread. In Luke Jesus offers the first cup before the blessing of the bread. There were four cups of wine offered at a Passover meal. Whether the Last Supper was on the day of Passover or the day before, as in John's Gospel, Jesus creatively uses the offering of the bread and wine as His body and blood. During a Passover meal the explanation of why this night is different from other nights is explained before the wine is drunk.

While Mark (14:24) and Matthew (26:28) mention "covenant" only Luke (22:20) among the Gospels has "new covenant." This is similar to Paul's explanation of the words of consecration (1 Cor 11:25). The cup of the "new covenant" establishes a new agreement between God and His people. Jeremiah in the following passage refers to the forthcoming "new covenant":

> The days are coming says the Lord, when I will make
> a new covenant with the house of Israel and the house

of Judah. It will not be like the covenant I made with their fathers the day I took them by the hand to lead them forth from the land of Egypt; for they broke My covenant and I had to show Myself their master, says the Lord. But this is the covenant which I will make with the house of Israel after those days, says the Lord. I will place My law within them, and write it upon their hearts: I will be their God, and they shall be My people. (Jr 31:31-33)

The new covenant is necessary because the old one was broken. And it is through the cup that the new covenant is made. The sharing of the cup is significant in that those who partake of it indicate a willingness to share in the suffering of Jesus. When John and James asked if they might sit one at the right and the other at the left of Jesus, He asked whether they would be willing to drink of the same cup as He, meaning to share in His suffering (Mk 10:38). That the cup is an indication of Jesus' suffering is also indicated when He asks the Father to remove the cup from Him, if it is the Father's will (Lk 22:42). Jesus said to Peter as He was being arrested, "Put your sword into its scabbard. Shall I not drink the cup the Father gave Me?" (Jn 18:11). The symbolism of those who drink the cup when it is offered is that they are willing to share in Jesus' suffering.

Sharing the same cup together is a sign of koinonia, or community, and of one's willingness to follow Jesus. Drinking from the same cup is also a sharing in the sufferings of each of the members of the community. The cup is not just an object, it is an action of sharing and commitment.

In offering the bread the words, "Do this in memory of Me" are peculiar to Luke (22:19) and to Paul (1 Cor 11:24); the latter also uses it in offering the cup. Luke says, "likewise" or "in the same way" but does not repeat, "in memory of Me." What is to be remembered here is the person of Jesus, His teachings, His sacrifice of Himself and His resurrection. The remembrance is to be done certainly in the Eucharistic meal but should not be restricted to it. Jesus is to be remembered at all meals and at all times. The remembrance is to be imbedded in the Christian psyche so that Jesus is first before mother or father, sister or brother, husband or wife, anyone and everything. The liturgical feast has special meaning for all are invited, rich or poor, whatever ethnic or racial background, male and female. This is a remembrance of the universal community in which Jesus is not only present in the bread and wine, offered and consumed, but is also unifying the community, as each partakes of Him, and His presence permeates the congregation.

## John's Gospel

The Gospel of John is the last written of the four Gospels. It is variously dated from 90 CE to 100 CE with chapter 21, a redaction, added later. While it has no words of institution, chapter six is a wonderful discourse on the "bread of life." There is little doubt that in it, Jesus is referring to the Eucharist. After the feeding of the five thousand by the multiplication of the five barley loaves and the two fish (6:5-15), the calming of the sea (6:16-21), and the following after Him of the people who were seeking more food (6:25-29), Jesus launches into a theological discourse on the bread from heaven (6:30-59). Jesus refers to Himself as "the bread of God… Who comes down from heaven and gives life to the world" (6:33). He is the "bread of life" and anyone who comes to Him "shall not hunger, and anyone who believes in (Him) shall never thirst" (6:35); "whoever eats this bread will live for ever" and the bread that He gives "for the life of the world" is His flesh (6:51).

Pope Benedict XVI, as Cardinal Ratzinger, wrote eloquently of the humble servant Jesus at the Passover supper in John's Gospel (13:1-7) when He washes His disciples' feet, preparing them for the meal:

> In the washing of the disciples' feet is represented for us what Jesus does and what He is. He, who is Lord comes down to us; He lays aside the garments of glory and becomes a slave, one who stands at the door and who does for us the slave's service of washing our feet. This is the meaning of His whole life and Passion: that He bends down to our dirty feet, to the dirt of humanity, and that in His greater love washes us clean. The slave's service of washing the feet was performed in order to prepare a person suitably for sitting at table, to make him ready for company, so that all could sit down together for a meal. Jesus Christ prepares us, as it were, for God's presence and for each other's company so that all could sit down together at table. (Ratzinger, 30)

## NEW TESTAMENT POST-RESURRECTION EUCHARISTIC MEALS

There are a dearth of post-resurrection meals mentioned in the Christian Scriptures. It may be that a reason for not describing more Eucharistic meals was that it was taken for granted that there would be a daily celebration of "breaking of bread" at home (Ac 2:42, 46-47). We have seen that Paul berated the Corinthian community on their attitude and conduct during the agape meal and separated that meal from the Eucharistic celebration (1 Corinthians 11:20-34). The Eucharist, however, continued to be celebrated in the house churches with and without preceding meals. What was necessary, according to Paul, is that the community be one, without divisions because of economic or other distinctions.

Jesus was present and presided at a meal at Emmaus. Cleopas and his companion invited Him to stay at their house because the hour was late.

> And it happened that while He was with them at table He took bread, said the blessing, broke it, and gave it to them. With that their eyes were opened and they recognized Him, but He vanished from their sight. Then they said to each other, "Were not our hearts burning within us while He spoke to us on the way and opened the Scriptures to us?" (Lk 24:30-32)

The disciples were rewarded for their hospitality by having a meal with Jesus. Jesus rewards hospitality by His presence. A hospitable, egalitarian atmosphere is a prerequisite in the worshiping community. It will also be noted that the explanation of Scripture preceded the meal and led to a proper understanding of Jesus' mission. Scriptural understanding must not be superficial but be taken into the depths of the heart. Again, the proclamation and explanation of Scripture necessarily precedes the "breaking of bread" in the liturgical celebration.

Paul emphasizes the necessity of unity in the Eucharistic celebration: "The cup of blessing that we bless, is it not a participation in the blood of Christ? The bread that we break, is it not a participation in the body of Christ? Because the loaf of bread is one, we though many, are one body, for we all partake of the one loaf" (1 Cor 10:16-17).

Jerome Murphy-O'Connor puts it succinctly: "Through sharing in the Body and Blood of Christ, believers are united with Him and with each other. The physical gesture of eating and drinking at the Christian sacred meal has the effect of bringing into being a new Body which is the physical presence of Christ in the world.... The physical gesture of eating and drinking adds a new dimension. Since all share in the one drink which is Christ and in the one bread which is Christ, Christ (to put it very crudely) becomes a possession which all hold in common, and are thereby forged into unity" (Murphy-O'Connor, *1 Corinthians*, 97).

One should add that there has to be a predisposition to unity which is then forged into the one unified body. The Eucharist does not automatically create unity without a desire for such unity on the part of the worshiping community. This necessity for koinonia is clearly indicated by Paul (1 Cor 11:20-34).

Another post-resurrection meal which Jesus had with His disciples was at the Sea of Tiberias (Lake Galilee). Seven of them had gone fishing but caught nothing all night long. At dawn Jesus cried out from the shore telling them to cast their net on the starboard side which resulted in a catch of one hundred and fifty-three fish. He had a charcoal fire going with some fish on it and some bread. He had them bring over some of the fish they caught to place on the fire and He invited them to breakfast. "Jesus came over and took the bread and gave it to them, and in like manner the fish" (Jn 21:1-13). One recalls the multiplication of the barley bread and fish to feed the five thousand (Jn 6:1-14). There are clear Eucharistic connotations in this meal by the sea. It is a reminder to the Johannine community that Jesus is present when they "break bread" together.

In the Acts of the Apostles, there is a clear Eucharistic celebration in Troas where there was a gathering on the Sabbath to "break bread." Paul gave a long discourse until midnight as a part of the gathering. After resuscitating a youth who, after falling asleep, fell from the third story of the building where they were gathered, Paul "went up and 'broke bread' and ate, continuing to discourse extensively until daybreak" (Ac 20:7-11). The long sermon preceded and continued after the "breaking of bread." It is clear that with Paul the logos (the word) surrounded and was essential to the celebration of the Eucharist.

## HOUSE CHURCHES

Roman architecture during Paul's time included apartment structures that reached five and six stories. The wealthy would live on the ground floor while the poorest would live on the top floor since there were five or six stories to climb. The apartments of the wealthy were more extensive and could entertain many more people then the apartments of the poor. There were also, of course, Christians with private unattached residences. When Paul gathered to "break bread" and gave his multi-hour sermon at Troas it was in an apartment complex. He apparently spoke from a courtyard and people were listening from their windows.

There are other references in the Christian Scriptures to "breaking bread" in homes. As already cited above: "Every day they devoted themselves to meeting together in the Temple area and to breaking bread in their homes. They ate their meals with exultation and sincerity of heart, praising God and enjoying favor with all the people" (Ac 2:46, 47a). These early Jerusalem Christians continued Jewish prayer practices, including attendance at the Temple and synagogue but separated the "breaking of the bread" which they did in their homes. The suggestion here is that they may not necessarily have gathered together as a Christian community each time "bread was broken," but that families may have "broken bread" individually at home, and that the community gathered together on the first day of the week. It also seems probable that those who lived in proximity, such as in an apartment complex, may have gathered to celebrate together. It does not appear that there were any hard and fast rules for "breaking bread" at this early stage, and there is no indication whether or not one of the Twelve was present at each celebration.

In the Letter to the Colossians we find reference to a house church: "Give greetings to the brothers (and sisters, adelphoi) in Laodicea and to Nympha and to the church in her house" (4:15). Nympha had a gathering of Christians in her house. Philemon had a church in his house (Phm 2). The early believers tended to meet in the houses of the more affluent since their homes would be larger and there would be more room for a gathering.

Prisca and Aquila had house churches both at Rome (Rm 16:5) and in the East. In his First Letter to the Corinthians Paul writes, "The churches of Asia send greetings, Aquila and Prisca together with the church at their house send you many greetings in the Lord" (16:19). Paul greets Prisca and Aquila, who moved back to Rome after the expulsion of the Jews was rescinded, "Greet Prisca and Aquila, my co-workers in Christ Jesus, who risked their necks to save my life, and not only I but also all the churches of the Gentiles thank them; greet also the church at their house" (Rm 16:3-5a). Prisca and Aquila established house churches in Corinth (where Paul worked with Aquila as tent makers), at Ephesus, and in Rome.

There were no church buildings for the early Christians. They met and celebrated in their homes. John Zizioulas in his published doctoral dissertation argues that the basic reason for gathering in the house churches was to celebrate the Eucharist and this is the reason for the linkage of church and home. He argues that there is a distinction between the Christian family and the notion of church. He indicates that all ecclesial activities could be performed outside of Christian houses such as preaching in synagogues but that the celebration of the Eucharist never took place outside of Christian homes. He argues that the term "house" and "church" expressed two different realities.

"House" expressed something secular while the Eucharist was a purely ecclesial reality (*Eucharist, Bishop, Church,* 51, 52).

The emphasis by Vatican II is on the family as the domestic church. Rather than secularize it and separate it from the official Church, the family needs theological support as an ecclesial part of the Church and as an integrated whole of its various parts. The domestic church is the beginning and underpinning of the universal Church. Zizioulas correctly indicates that when the Eucharist was celebrated in the house of a Christian family the Church was automatically linked to that household and the term "the Church in the household" of that Christian family was applied. More correctly it was named after the leader(s) of that family rather than the family name per se. There was more, however, in the celebration of the Eucharist. There was fellowship, moral and economic support, a social gathering, a bodily meal. As a fledgling group beset by opposition there was a need for solidarity and mutual support. All this was part of the gathering for the celebration of the Eucharist.

**The Christian Meal**

Jesus is present at every meal in which He is invoked. He is always the ultimate host. Even when He is a guest in the many meals He partakes of in Luke's Gospel, He is the host. Christian meals transcend space and time even though they are human events. The memories, the commitments, the joys of human meals can transcend space and time. When Eucharistic devotions were cut off from the Christian meals some of the meaning was lost. This is not to suggest that the Church's Eucharist should be returned to a simple meal but that the Sabbath celebration as developed over the centuries should be related to the family meal with the latter fulfilling some of the deep social needs of a table gathering.

Pope Benedict XVI correctly rejects the notion that the Eucharistic celebration should be returned to a simple meal: "The historical development of the Church's Eucharist is not a decline from its origins but the true fruit of those origins. Those attempts to tell us that we should 'get back' to a simple profane meal, to multipurpose areas and so on, are only in appearance a return to the origins. In reality, they are a step back behind the *turning point of the Cross and the Resurrection*, that is, behind the essentials that are the basis for Christianity in all its novelty. This is not restoring the original state, but abandoning the mystery of Easter and, thereby, the very center of the mystery of Christ" (Ratzinger, 65). The beautiful liturgies developed by Eastern Orthodoxy and Roman Catholicism give glory to God and lift the human spirit.

Pope John Paul II's legacy in this regard is that each Christian household is called to be a church in miniature, an *ecclesia domestica*. The family as a communion of persons should be an efficacious and fruitful sign mirroring the loving union between Christ and the Church (*America*, 4/18/05).

Sharing a meal together with adequate prayer and remembrance is in continuity with the Lord's Supper. The sharing of food at home with prayer and support, community and commitment is a satellite of the liturgical celebration. While there is no consecration and the Lord is not present in the food elements, and there is not the universal invitation to all, He is present because He has been called upon. "For where two or three are gathered together in My name, there am I in the midst of them" (Mt 18:20).

There are foundational historical precedents for a liturgical relationship in the meal at home. As we have seen, the family meal was important for Jewish worship and devotion. The Sabbath family meals were liturgical type celebrations. The Jewish meal was a sacred act with praise of God for the gifts given. The first Jerusalem Christians, who were Jews, followed this practice: "Every day they devoted themselves to meeting together in the Temple area and to breaking bread in their homes. They ate their meals with exultation and sincerity of heart, praising God and enjoying favor with all the people" (Ac 2:46, 47a).

Vatican II calls the family "the primary vital cell of society," and, "by the mutual affection of its members and by family prayer, presents itself as a domestic sanctuary of the Church" (*Decree on the Apostolate of Lay People*, III, 11). The family "constitutes the basis of society" (*Pastoral Constitution on the Church in the Modern World*, I, 52). Vatican II calls the family, "the domestic church" (Ibid., I, 11). *The Catechism of the Catholic Church* develops this concept further: "The Christian family constitutes a specific revelation and realization of ecclesial communion, and for this reason it can and should be called a *domestic church*. It is a community of faith, hope, and charity; it assumes singular importance in the Church, as is evident in the New Testament" (2204).

The early Christians met "in the household of...," that is, in Christian homes, to celebrate the Eucharist. It was in someone's house that the Eucharist was celebrated, preceded by the agape meal. There is, therefore, a foundational basis for celebration in the domestic church.

A theology of the relationship between the liturgical celebration and the Christian meal is needed. There is great need today to strengthen the family. The family's umbilical cord is tied to the liturgical Sabbath Eucharistic celebration. The importance of eating together, calling upon the Lord's presence, and the relationship of the meal to the Sunday celebration, needs to be developed and catechized. Suggested prayers and conduct should be developed by the Church for family use.

Just as the Jewish family meal, particularly the Sabbath meal, was a sacred meal because it was related to the Passover celebration, in a similar way, the Christian family meal should theologically be related to the Eucharistic celebration. The Israelite household, wherever it is located, is treated as comparable to the Temple in cultic activity. Although there is contradiction in the Torah, the household is the place where the Passover may be observed (Pelikan, 2005, 81). Since Christianity depends so much on Jewish cultic practices, careful study should be made as to what practices the universal Church should develop and encourage for the domestic church.

The Sunday liturgical gathering, unlike the family meal, is a universal invitation to all baptized believers, male and female, rich or poor, young or old, and all national, ethnic and racial backgrounds. The family meal lacks the universal invitation, but family members imbued with community prayer, the word and the sacrament at the Sabbath gathering, call upon the presence of the Lord at the family meal with a direct umbilical connection between the two celebrations.

## PRAYERS & PRESIDER(S)
## AT THE EUCHARISTIC GATHERING

Who presided at the churches which met in the houses of Nympha, Philemon, Prisca and Aquila and the many other house churches where Christians met? No one is named in the Scriptures as presider. When Paul "broke bread" at Troas it is probable that he presided although he is not specifically named as presider (Ac 20:12). Zizioulas assumes that Paul presided and, from this, concludes that we are obliged to accept that when the Apostles were present they presided (*Eucharist...*, 62).

It certainly was not possible for the Twelve, or Paul, Barnabas, Timothy and Titus to be present and lead each house church in the celebration of the "breaking of the bread." The house churches in a particular locale would probably have met together for the "first day of the week" and on special occasions at which time an authorized person would lead the celebration. In the places that Paul, and his two main assistants, Timothy and Titus visited, they would appoint elders to head those churches. Some places such as Jerusalem and Antioch would have a more mature developed ecclesia while other places, particularly those in new and outlying areas, would not. Christianity was spreading very quickly and there were various stages of development.

### St. Ignatius of Antioch

At the beginning of the second century (106 CE) the letters to the various churches by St. Ignatius of Antioch refer specifically to bishops, presbyters and deacons. Without these, Ignatius says, there can be no church. The presbyters, at this time, can be likened to an advisory council: "Correspondingly, everyone must show the deacons respect. They represent Jesus Christ, just as the bishop has the role of the Father, and the presbyters are like God's council and an apostolic band. You cannot have a church without these" (*Trallians* 3:1).

With respect to the Eucharist, Ignatius urges frequent celebrations: "Try to gather together more frequently to celebrate God's Eucharist and to praise Him. For when you meet with frequency, Satan's powers are overthrown and his destructiveness is undone by the unanimity of your faith" (*Ephesians* 13:1).

There were traveling prophets as well as competing gatherings, but Ignatius urges that there be one Eucharist with the bishop, presbytery and deacons: "Be careful then to observe a single Eucharist. For there is one flesh of our Lord, Jesus Christ, and one cup of His blood that makes us pure, and one altar, just as there is one bishop along with the presbytery and the deacons, my fellow slaves. In that whatever you do is in line with God's will" (*Philadelphians* 4).

It is the bishop, or someone he designates, who can preside at Eucharist: "You should regard that Eucharist as authentic which is presided over either by the bishop or by someone he authorizes. Where the bishop is present, there let the congregation gather, just as where Jesus Christ is, there is the Catholic Church" (*Smyrnaeans* 8:1, 2).

In his letters to the Ephesians, Magnesians, Trallians, Philadelphians, and Smyrnaeans, Ignatius refers to bishops, presbyters and deacons but in his letter to the Romans he does not mention any church hierarchy. His main concern in his letter to the Romans is that no one intercede for him to save him from his impending martyrdom.

## The *Didache* (The Teaching of the Twelve Apostles)

The *Didache* (or "teaching" in Greek) is an early Greek manuscript discovered by the Greek Orthodox Archbishop Philotheos Byrennios in 1873. There is dispute among scholars as to its dating with some believing that the document has a knowledge of Matthew and Luke (middle 80's CE) and the *Shepherd* of Hermas (about 100 CE). Others also believe that there were redactions along the way so that there are later additions.

Aaron Milavec in his recent massive study of *The Didache: Faith, Hope & Life of the Earliest Christian Communities, 50-70 CE* argues effectively for a mid first century date. He believes that the document has a distinct unity, composed independently of any Gospel and is a program used for the formation of a Gentile entering Christianity. The Eucharistic prayers in chapters 9 and 10 are fashioned after the Jewish forms for grace before and after meals and indicate that the celebration was still a real supper:

9. Now about the Eucharist: This is how to give thanks: First in connection with the cup:

"We thank You, Father, for the holy vine of David, Your child, which You have revealed through Jesus, Your Child. To You be glory forever."

Then in connection with the piece (broken off the loaf):

"We thank You, our Father, for the life and knowledge which You have revealed through Jesus, Your Child. To You be glory forever.

As this piece (of bread) was scattered over the hills and then was brought together from the ends of the earth into Your kingdom. For Yours is the glory and the power through Jesus Christ forever."

You must not let anyone eat or drink of your Eucharist except those baptized in the Lord's name. For in reference to this the Lord said, "Do not give what is sacred to dogs."

10. After you have finished your meal, say grace in this way:

"We thank You holy Father, for Your sacred name which You have lodged in our hearts, and for the knowledge and faith and immortality which You have revealed through Jesus, Your Child. To You be glory forever.

Almighty Master, You have created everything for the sake of Your name, and have given men food and drink to enjoy that they may thank You. But to us You have given spiritual food and drink and eternal life through Jesus, Your Child.

Above all we thank You that You are mighty. To You be glory forever.

Remember Lord, Your Church, save it from all evil and make it perfect by Your love. Make it holy, and gather it together from the four winds into Your kingdom which You have ready for it. For Yours is the power and the glory forever.

Let Grace come and let this world pass away.
Hosanna to the God of David!
If anyone is holy let him come. If not let him repent.
Our Lord, come!
Amen."
In the case of prophets. however, you should let them give
thanks in their own way.

In the *Didache* communities, apostles and prophets were
welcomed and given hospitality for one day and in case of necessity two days. If he stayed three days he was considered a false
prophet. On departing an apostle or prophet could not accept
anything except sufficient food to carry to his next destination.
If he asked for money he was considered a false prophet (11:3-
6). Anyone who came "in the name of the Lord" had to be welcomed. A traveler should be helped but could not stay more than
two days or if necessary three. If he desired to settle in the community and had a trade he must work for his living. If he had no
trade judgment had to be used that he not live as an idle Christian (12:1-4).

In addition to prophets and teachers who minister, the community is also urged to elect bishops and deacons "who are a credit
to the Lord, men who are gentle, generous, faithful and well tried.
For their ministry to you is identical with that of the prophets
and teachers" (15:1).

## Justin the Martyr

The first description of a Christian liturgy comes from Justin
the martyr, a layman, who taught a form of Christian wisdom at
Rome, around 150 CE.

He described two celebrations of the Eucharist: the first
emphasized the newly converted; and the second, a Sunday celebration. In his *First Apology* he describes the first situation:

After we have thus cleansed the person who believes and has joined our ranks, we lead him to where those we call "brothers" are assembled to offer prayers in common for ourselves, for him who has just been enlightened, and for all men everywhere. It is our desire, now that we have come to know the truth, to be found worthy of doing good deeds and obeying the commandments, and thus to obtain eternal salvation. When we have finished praying, we greet one another with a kiss. Then bread and a cup containing water and wine mixed with water are brought to him who presides over the brethren; he takes them and offers prayers, glorifying the Father of all things through the name of the Son and the Holy Spirit; and he utters a lengthy thanksgiving because the Father has judged us worthy of these gifts. When the prayer of thanksgiving is ended, all the people present give their assent with an "Amen!" ("Amen" in Hebrew means "so be it"). When the president has given thanks and the people have all signified their assent those whom we call "deacons" distribute the bread and the wine and water, over which the thanksgiving has been spoken, to each of those present; they also carry them to those who are absent. (ch. 65)

This food we call "Eucharist" and no one may share it unless he believes that our teaching is true, and has been cleansed in the bath of forgiveness for sin and rebirth, and lives as Christ taught. For we do not receive these things as though they were ordinary food and drink. Just as Jesus Christ our Savior was made flesh through the word of God and took flesh and blood for our salvation, so too (we have been taught) through the word of prayer that comes from Him the food over which the thanksgiving has been spoken becomes the flesh and blood of the incarnate Jesus, in order to nourish and transform our flesh and blood. For, in the memoirs which the apostles composed and which we call "Gospels," they have told us that they were commissioned thus: Jesus took bread and, having given thanks, said: "Do this in memory of Me; this is My body"; and in like manner He took the cup and having given thanks said: "This is My blood," and He gave these to them alone. Wicked demons have taught men to imitate all this in the mysteries of Mithras. For, as you know or can find out, there too bread and a cup of water are presented when someone is being initiated in the sacred rites, and meanwhile certain words are spoken. (ch. 66)

Since that time we constantly recall these events among ourselves; if we have anything, we help all who are in need, and we are constantly united with one another. And for all that we eat we thank the Maker of all through His Son Jesus Christ and the Holy Spirit. And on the day named after the sun, all who live in city or countryside assemble, and the memoirs of the apostles or the writings of the prophets are read as long as time allows. When the lector has finished, the president addresses us, admonishing us and exhorting us to imitate the splendid things we have heard. Then we all stand and pray, and, as we said earlier, when we have finished praying, bread, wine, and water are brought up. The president offers prayers of thanksgiving, according to his ability, and the people give their assent with an "Amen!" Next, the gifts over which the thanksgiving has been spoken are distributed, and each one shares in them, while they are also sent via the deacon to the absent brethren. The wealthy who are willing make contributions, each as he pleases, and the collection is deposited with the president who aids orphans and widows, those who are in want because of sickness or some other reason, those in prison, and visiting strangers; in short, he takes care of all in need. The reason we all assemble on Sunday is that it is the first day; the day on which God transformed darkness and matter and created the world, and the day on which Jesus Christ our Savior rose from the dead. (ch. 67)

It appears that Justin is describing a Eucharist which immediately follows Baptism and a Sunday Eucharist. It will be noted that in this discourse addressed to pagans, the celebrant is referred to as "the one presiding," "he who presides," or "the president." The only other titles mentioned are the "deacons" who distribute the Eucharist to those present and take it to those not present, and the "lector" who reads from the Scriptures.

## *Apostolic Tradition* of Hippolytus

The *Apostolic Tradition* of Hippolytus (early 3rd century) provides the first extant complete Eucharistic prayer. It was a guide, not a required set prayer. It had great influence in its own time and was the basis for contemporary efforts to renew the Eucharist (Osborne). By this time it is the bishop who presides.

Let us offer the kiss of peace to him who has been made a bishop, saluting him because he has been made worthy. Let the deacons present the oblation to him,

and after placing his hands on it, along with the entire presbytery, let him give thanks:

The Lord be with you.
And let all say: and with your spirit (2 Tm 4:22).
(Let us lift) up our hearts.
We have them (lifted) to the Lord.
Let us give thanks to the Lord.
It is fitting and right (2 Th 1:3).

And then let him continue as follows:

We give thanks to You, O God, through Your beloved
servant Jesus Christ, whom You have sent to us in the
last times (Gal 4:4) as Savior and Redeemer and Angel of Your will (Is 9:5). He is Your inseparable Word,
through whom You have created all things (Jn 1:3),
and in Him You were well pleased (Mt 3:17). You sent
Him from heaven into the womb of the Virgin, and
He, dwelling in the womb, was made flesh, and was
manifested as Your Son, born of the Holy Spirit and
the Virgin.

When He had fulfilled Your will, and obtained (Ac
20:28) a holy people (1 P 2:9) for You, He stretched
forth His hands when He suffered, that He might free
from suffering those who believed in You.

When He was handed over to His voluntary suffering, that He might destroy death, and burst the bonds
of the devil, and tread upon the nether world, and il-
lumine the just, and fix the limit, and reveal the Resurrection, taking bread, He gave thanks to You, and
said: Take eat, this is My body which will be broken
for you.

Similarly also the cup, saying: This is My blood which is shed for you. When you do this, you are making a remembrance of Me.

Wherefore remembering His death and Resurrection, we offer to You the bread and the cup, giving thanks to You because You have accounted us worthy to stand in Your presence and serve You. And we ask that You send Your Holy Spirit upon the oblation of Holy Church, and that gathering it together into one, You grant to all who partake of the holy things a fullness of the Holy Spirit for the strengthening of faith in truth, that we may praise You and glorify You through Your servant Jesus Christ, through whom be glory and honor to You, to the Father and to the Son with the Holy Spirit in Your Holy Church, both now, and unto the ages of ages. Amen.

In the third century while there was a trend toward uniformity in the Church there were differences in local practices, each church basing their practices on apostolic teaching. The *Apostolic Tradition* (8) describes the first ordination of a presbyter. The bishop lays his hands on the head of the one to be ordained while the presbyters touch him. A presbyter does not ordain but seals while the bishop ordains. In his prayer the bishop asks that the new presbyter be given "the spirit of grace and counsel" to "sustain and govern" the people.

### The Role of the Bishop

Vatican II discussed the power of bishops (*Christus Dominus*, 2, 4, 5, 8a, 8b). They are the successor to the Apostles (Ibid., 2, 4, 6, 8, 20). It states, "Since the apostolic office of bishops *was instituted by Christ the Lord* and is directed to a spiritual and supernatural end, the sacred Ecumenical Council asserts that the competent ecclesiastical authority has the proper, special, and as of right, exclusive power to appoint and install bishops" (Ibid., 20).

It is the consistent teaching of the Church that bishops are the successors to and carry on the work of the apostles. Vatican II says it emphatically, "...it proposes to proclaim publicly and enunciate clearly the doctrine concerning bishops, successors of the apostles, who together with Peter's successor, the Vicar of Christ and the visible head of the whole Church, direct the house of the living God" (*Lumen Gentium*, 18).

The emphasis on the powers and the authority of the bishop in *Christus Dominus* is put in perspective: "Sent as he is by the Father to govern his family, a bishop should keep before his eyes the example of the Good Shepherd, who came not to be served but to serve (Mt 20:28; Mk 10:25) and to lay down his life for his sheep (Jn 10:11)" (LG, 27). "Through the power of the Holy Spirit they are to witness to Christ through *diakonia*. That office, however, which the Lord committed to the pastors of his people, is, in the strict sense of the term, a service, which is called very expressively in sacred Scripture a *diakonia* or ministry (Ac 1:17, 25; 21:19; Rm 11:13; 1 Tm 1:12)" (LG, 24).

The functions of a bishop include:

1. Preaching the Gospel which has pride of place (LG, 25).
2. Collectively having the privilege of infallibility in (a) teaching on matters of faith and morals which are held definitively and absolutely, and (b) when assembled in ecumenical council (Ibid.).
3. Being a steward of the Eucharist which he offers or ensures is offered and exercises in a supreme degree his sacred function (LG, 26, 28).
4. Controlling the conferring of Baptism (Ibid.).
5. Being the original minister of Confirmation (Ibid.).
6. Governing the particular church assigned to him (LG, 27).

"It is bishops who enjoy the fullness of the sacrament of orders, and both priests and deacons are dependent on them in the exercise of their power. The former, in order that they may be prudent cooperators with the episcopal order, have also been consecrated as true priests of the New Testament; the latter, having been ordained for the ministry, serve the people of God in union with the bishop and his clergy" (*Christus Dominus*, 15).

The Vatican II decree emphasizes the power and the authority of the bishop, his relationship to his priests and to the faithful who are to be encouraged to "Catholic action" (Ibid., 17). The "Eucharistic Sacrifice is the center and culmination of the entire life of the Christian community" (Ibid., 2). Parish priests are to ensure its celebration. Each diocese "should normally have enough priests capable of looking after the People of God" (Ibid., 3).

Since the early second century the Eucharist celebrated by the bishop was the central act of the koinonia. Ignatius of Antioch emphasizes that there can be only one Eucharist celebrated by the one bishop (*Phil.* 4:2). As indicated above, for Ignatius the Eucharist is authentic only when it is presided over by the bishop or someone he authorizes (*Smyr.* 8:1).

The bishop's role in the celebration of the Eucharist was considered so important that later when presbyters presided in outlying communities, a portion of the Eucharistic bread consecrated by the bishop was placed in the chalice (*The New Dictionary of Theology*, 135).

The role and the functions of bishops have not been consistent throughout the centuries. Yves Congar addresses this question: "The episcopate... has taken more than one form, and it has been lived in very different styles. Because the episcopate, as authority and as sacrament, is always the same, we are inclined to overlook the gulf that separates the leader of a community in the early Church, a bishop of feudal times, and a twentieth century pastor. The Church and the priesthood are of all time; but they are also the Church of today, the priesthood of today.... Through familiarity with historical forms we can distinguish more clearly the permanence of the essential and the variety of forms; we can locate the absolute and the relative more exactly, and so better remain true to the absolute while we shape the relative to the needs of the time" (Congar, 1964, 14).

## DISTRIBUTION OF THE EUCHARIST

In 2003, Pope John Paul II released an encyclical, *Ecclesia de Eucharistia* (*On the Eucharist in Its Relationship to the Church*: EE). The challenge to the Catholic Church is to stress the importance of the Eucharist, to feed the lambs, to tend and feed the sheep (Jn 21:15-17), certainly with the Word, but also, most importantly, with the Body and Blood of the Lord. Who will do the feeding — both of those at church services and of those who do not attend — is the continuing challenge to the Church. The celebration of the Holy Sacrifice of the Mass, to be valid, requires the celebrant be either a bishop or a priest (EE 32). However, those distributing Holy Communion at Mass include, in addition to the ordained, extraordinary ministers of the Eucharist. Many Catholics who do not attend Mass, or attend Mass infrequently, invariably and eventually wind up in hospitals and nursing homes or become home bound. Here again the primary Church representatives who minister to them in the United States are lay persons with deacons undoubtedly as the most frequent ordained ministers who visit the sick. While chaplains, parish priests and deacons also visit the sick, the sheer number of the ill and infirm necessitates the need for extraordinary ministers of the Eucharist. While deacons can administer Viaticum to the dying, only priests or bishops can administer the Sacrament of the Sick.

In the early Church it was the deacon who brought the Eucharist to the sick and homebound. While the deacon is an ordinary minister of Holy Communion, and the number of deacons has increased considerably, they are involved in many other ministries and the Church must rely on lay extraordinary ministers to visit the sick and homebound. The hospital bed, nursing home and the house of the homebound are crossroads for evangelization, and in particular, for the many who have been infrequent or lapsed Mass attendees, the divorced and remarried, and those confined to prisons.

Vatican II in its "Decree on the Apostolate of Lay Persons" (*Apostolicum Actuositatem*) recalls how spontaneous and fruitful the layman's vocation was in the early Church. It points out the responsibility of the lay person to carry on the apostolate (1), the sharing of the laity in the priestly, prophetic and kingly office of Christ (2, 10), and the lay person's responsibility in the apostolate of evangelization (6). Because of need and the ability, zeal, education and training of many lay persons in the United States, they are increasingly contributing to parish activities, emulating the experience of the early Church. With respect to the Eucharist the laity are becoming increasingly visible in the distribution of Holy Communion both at church services and to those not able to attend Mass.

# VI

---

# THEOSIS (Θεοσις) AND
# THE HOLY EUCHARIST

The early Greek Fathers of the Church saw humankind as gradually being brought to the likeness of Jesus Christ. It is a spiritual ascent to God.

According to Clement of Alexandria, the teacher of Christian doctrine has the task of leading the faithful to the imitation of God and His Logos Who are the real teachers. The simple believer is to be led through study and asceticism to the elimination of vices and passions to a state of *apatheia* and to *gnosis*, the knowledge of divine secrets. The believer thus becomes equal to the angels in his knowledge of God's truths. The final step in this spiritual ascent is a possession, by anticipation, theosis, the assimilation to the Logos, and union with God. To Clement the Eucharist is important primarily for its effects on this process.

There is thus an analogy between the mingling of the wine and the water and the mingling of man and the Pneuma (Spirit): the first mingling, that of wine and water, is a festive meal given for the sake of faith; in the other mingling, the Pneuma leads man to incorruptibility. The mingling of the two, that is, of the drink and the Logos, is called Eucharist, a grace that is praised for its beauty. Those who share in it with faith are sanctified in body and soul, when the Father's

will mysteriously mingles with man, this divine mix-
ture, with the Pneuma and the Logos. In truth the
Pneuma is closely related to the soul which it draws
along, and the flesh is closely related to the Logos, the
flesh on account of which the Logos became flesh.
(*The Eucharist of the Early Christians*, 114)

In his writings Clement seems to accept the ancient Christian idea that the Eucharistic flesh and blood results in the physical preservation of the body of the recipient.

Maximus says that "No creature is capable of deification by
its own nature since it is not capable of grasping God. This can
happen only by the grace of God"; and, with regard to the free
will participation of the human being, "…the spirit does not gen-
erate a will that is not willing, but he transforms into deification
a will that has desire" (J. Pelikan, Vol. II, 11, 12).

Irenaeus, who became bishop of Lyons, also alludes to man
growing closer in likeness to God by becoming incorruptible
through the Eucharist:

For the bread that comes from the earth, when it receives the invocation of God is no longer ordinary
bread but the Eucharist which comprises two elements, an earthly and a heavenly, so our bodies which
participate in the Eucharist are no longer corruptible,
since they now have the hope of resurrection. (*Against
Heresies* 4, 18, 5; *Eucharist…*, 91)

For Irenaeus, "The glory of God gives life; those who see
God receive life. For this reason God, Who cannot be grasped,
comprehended or seen allows Himself to be seen, comprehended
and grasped by men, that He may give life to those who see and
receive Him" (*Against Heresies*, 4, 20, 5-7: SC 100, 640-642, 644-
648).

Irenaeus sees man, whose humble origins began with a breath by God into clay (Gn 2:7), is meant to develop into a perfect state. Our body "is sown in corruption but rises incorrupt" (1 Cor 15:42). The Eucharist teaches us to welcome "the Spirit who perfects and prepares us for incorruptibility and gradually accustoms us to receiving God" (Ibid. 5, 8, 1; *Eucharist...*, 96). Man is caught up in this universal ascent as he makes himself part of the Eucharistic sacrifice which comes from the Father and returns to Him. "Man advances slowly and steadily to his perfection, to the encounter with God that will make him incorruptible. 'All who have the Spirit of God are led to the Word, that is, the Son, and the Son accepts them and offers them to His Father, and the Father bestows incorruptibility on them'" (Ibid., 4, 38, 1; *Eucharist...*, 97).

Gregory of Nyssa sees man as never satiated in his thirst for knowledge of God. The more knowledge he receives of God the greater his desire for more in a never satiated thirst that is basic to human nature. Gregory's concept of the destiny of man is a continuous and never ending ascent in the knowledge of God through communion in divine life.

Origen's απokαταστασις παντον (the restoration of all things) is an evolutionary concept of all things being eventually drawn to God, "for the end is like the beginning." It sees God's creation as being restored to its original beauty. Origen believed he was thinking within the confines of orthodoxy but his version of universalism was eventually condemned in the sixth century, a major reason being that he left no room for hell. Origen nevertheless contributes to the concept of the evolving process to God where there will be "a new heaven and a new earth," and all things will be made new (Rv 21:1, 5).

St. John Chrysostom indicates that the baptized Christian is not only born of God but has put on Christ; and this is not only morally through charity but in reality. The Incarnation (ensarkosis) has rendered our incorporation into Christ and our divinization (theosis) possible.

Karl Rahner gives modern theological language to the theosis introduced by the Greek Fathers. Rahner's evolutionary theory of intrinsic grace begins at creation and continues throughout human history. According to Rahner there is a transcendentality of the human mind, elevated by supernatural grace, which is open to the self-communication of God. Even without direct reflection, the dynamism directed toward the self-communication of God can be present in consciousness and have an effect upon man's individual and collective mental history. God's supernatural will is at all times directed to the salvation of all human beings and the offer of supernatural grace is always present whether grace is accepted or not. This does not mean that man is always conscious of this presence since God speaks and reveals Himself when He wills to whom He wills and in the manner He wills. Grace then can be accepted or rejected consciously or not consciously, the latter presumably depending on the state of the person's receptivity.

Because of God's will to save all human beings and because of the presence of the supernatural grace of Christ in all men, every self-communication of God may be called revelation even though it occurs in the transcendental and not yet reflective human consciousness. This points to Rahner's doctrine of the "anonymous Christian." These are human beings who by their free will have accepted the grace offered them in faith and charity even though they may not profess to be Christians. The term "anonymous Christian" is not a name to be given to others but is a way for Christians to look on others.

Spirit and matter in a human being have more things in common than they have differentiating them. They are mutually related and inseparable elements of the single person. While there is an essential difference between the two, they are not in opposition or mutually indifferent to each other. The intrinsic nature of the body is to develop towards spirit. This self-transcendence involves transcendence into "something substantially new, a leap to something essentially higher" (*Foundations of Christian Faith*, 184-185). Rahner coins the term "essential self-transcendence" to describe the process whereby something which existed earlier surpasses itself in order to become something different without losing itself (Ibid., 186).

The evolution of matter into spirit is generated by the spirit. While they are different, matter and spirit have an intrinsic co-ordination as both were created by the same God. They are distinct but not separate. This so-called "essential self-transcendence" not only results in a change beyond human power but, in becoming part of God through union with Him, still retains the essential self. The result is θεοσις (theosis) or divinization. God, out of love, created for the purpose of sharing life. Since all things in heaven and on earth are created by the same God, the essential self is not lost in this transcendence. The soul, therefore, according to Rahner cannot be separated from the body. The union with God can never be surpassed. In Jesus Christ the absolute self-communication of God is absolutely received.

It is in this evolutionary process of God's self-communication in grace that Jesus Christ appears in human history as the climax of the complete self-emptying (Ph 2:7) and complete acceptance of the self-communication of God. As Rahner puts it, "It is precisely this beginning of the irreversible and successful history of salvation which we are calling the absolute Savior, and hence in this sense this beginning is the fullness of time, and it is the end of the previous history of salvation and revelation which was, as it were still open" (Ibid., 194). The absolute Savior is part of the history of the cosmos. It is the climax or the highest point of that history.

In this sense Rahner is following the emphasis of the

Alexandrians (Clement, Origen) and the Cappadocians (Basil, Gregory of Nazianzus, Gregory of Nyssa) in emphasizing the Incarnation. Rahner does not directly relate the Incarnate Logos to the Eucharist in his exposition on the evolution of man to God through grace. It is true that grace, as Rahner describes it, is present and self-communicates independent of the Eucharist; hence the opportunity of the "anonymous Christian," because of God's free and gratuitous gift of Himself in grace, to evolve in the process of theosis. However, the Christian through the same self-communication of God is invited to the Eucharistic table where the absolute Savior's manhood and Godhood are offered through the power of the Holy Spirit.

Rahner's contributions have a mediating influence when he melds grace as an intrinsic part of humanity and grace as an absolute gratuity of God. This mediating spirit is present in an ecumenical sense as well when Rahner cross-fertilizes Eastern and Western theology as indicated by the Eastern Orthodox theologian J. Meyendorff:

"Rahner is melding Greek patristic and Western theology which includes the conclusion that man does not disappear in contact with God but, on the contrary, becomes more truly and freely man, not only in his similarity to God, but also in what makes him radically different than his Creator. According to Rahner 'each nature keeps its property… but shows precisely how it enters into the constitution of the united unity as an intrinsic factor, in such a way that unity and distinction become mutually conditioning and intensifying characteristics not competing ones'" (J. Meyendorff, *Byzantine Theology*, 211-212).

When we offer ourselves as nothing, that is, as empty, then we can be filled with Him Who is all. We can then become a part of Him, that is, more like Him, but still retain our unique nature. In order to die to ourselves and live with Christ, we must take leave of all we possess (Lk 14:33). There is a synthesis of the historical and the eschatological, that is, with the Jesus Who took on human flesh, and the Jesus Who ever was, is, and ever shall be, the Jesus Who represents us before the Father as our high priest. Just as Jesus emptied Himself to become one of us (Ph 2:7), we too empty ourselves to become one with Him. This emptying and filling can be realized most fully in the Eucharist. When we receive Holy Communion worthily and regularly, that which we receive, the living Christ, becomes fructified, becomes a part of us, remains with us, blossoms, bears fruit and returns to its infinite source. This is the theosis effect of the Eucharist. Bishop Kallistos Ware expresses the Orthodox view: "It is above all through Communion that the Christian is made one with and in Christ, 'christified,' 'ingodded,' or deified'; it is above all through Communion that he receives the first fruits of eternity" (Ware, *The Orthodox Way*, 146).

The process of theosis is without life and cannot be attained without the love of God flowing through the human being who expresses himself in charity and service to others. Greek Orthodox Metropolitan Anthony of San Francisco expressed it well in his last encyclical before he passed on to the Lord on Christmas day, 2004: "…Yet this process of theosis is not a matter of a discarnate spirituality that retreats from human need and suffering. The journey toward theosis is rather expressed through concrete acts of love and mercy in imitation of God who is love. As St. Gregory the Theologian writes, 'Prove yourself a god to the unfortunate, imitating the mercy of God. There is nothing as godly in human beings as to do good works'" (*Orthodox Observer*, Jan., 2005).

The Eucharist then is not merely food for our soul but strengthens us and prompts us to perform charitable works for those in need and in this process we imitate God and become more and more like Him.

# VII

# EUCHARIST AND UNITY
# EAST AND WEST

The Eucharist is unifying because those who partake of it partake of the same body and blood of the Savior. The same blood flows through the Christians of the East and the West, and they are brothers and sisters of the Lord and of each other. Differences began to emerge, however, between believers and nonbelievers and within the community. Let us state and restate some of the differences in the early Church to show that differences within the believing community are not unusual.

In the beginning there was one Christian Church. The first Christians huddled together to preserve and renew their faith. As indicated above, the early Christians who were Jews believed that Jesus was the anointed one and that their faith was a natural development within Judaism. They met together as believers and also attended the synagogue, the Temple, and followed Jewish practices (Ac 2:46). "The community of believers was of one heart and mind..." (Ac 4:32). After Stephen's martyrdom a severe persecution led by the Jewish authorities broke out and the believers were scattered throughout Judea and Samaria (Ac 8:1). Herod also began persecuting the believers because he saw it was pleasing to some of the Jews (Ac 12:1-4). Eventually those who followed Christ either left or were asked to leave the synagogue.

As Gentiles became believers there were differences between the Jewish believers in Jerusalem and the Gentile believers in Antioch and elsewhere with regard to following Mosaic practices. The synod of Jerusalem determined that the converted Gentiles did not have to undergo circumcision (Ac 15:28, 29). There nevertheless was tension between the Jerusalem church and the Antiochean and other churches with regard to dietary and other Mosaic practices.

Paul censured Peter because, when Jews from Jerusalem came to Antioch, Peter ceased to eat with the Gentiles "because he was afraid of the circumcised" (Gal 2:12). The connotation here, as indicated above, is that Peter, Barnabas and the visiting Jerusalem believers did not break (the Eucharistic) bread together with the Gentile converts. Paul called Peter and the others to task for their hypocrisy (Gal 2:13-14).

After an argument whether Mark should accompany them on the second evangelistic journey, Paul and Barnabas separated (Ac 15:39) and the two great missionaries did not team up together again.

There was also dissension within the Corinthian church. Some said they followed Paul, others Apollos, others Peter, others Christ. Paul asked the question, "Is Christ divided?" (1 Cor 1:12, 13). He pointed out to the Corinthians that they are of one body because of the Eucharist, "The cup of blessing that we bless, is it not participation in the blood of Christ? The bread that we break is it not a participation in the body of Christ? Because the loaf of bread is one, we, though many, are one body, for we all partake of the one loaf" (1 Cor 10:16, 17).

Ignatius of Antioch implored the faithful for unity, in his letters to the various churches. Visiting charismatics and prophets were drawing the people away from the community celebration. During this period of the early second century there were also probably various house churches within a particular community which had their allegiance to the leaders of those churches. The development of the mono episkopos (one bishop) would naturally present problems for them.

As pointed out above, Ignatius implored the people to celebrate with their bishop, "Run off, all of you, to one community of God, as it were, to one altar, to one Jesus Christ, Who came forth from one Father, while still remaining one with Him, and returned to Him." Again with respect to the bishop, "For when you obey the bishop as if he were Jesus Christ, you are (as I see it) living not in a merely human fashion but in Jesus Christ's way.... It is essential, therefore, to act in no way without the bishop" (*Trall.* 2:1).

There was controversy over the Eucharist from the beginning. In John's Gospel Jesus said, "'I am the living bread that came down from heaven; whoever eats this bread will live forever; and the bread that I will give is My flesh for the life of the world.... Whoever eats My flesh and drinks My blood has eternal life, and I will raise him up on the last day.' As a result many of His disciples said, 'This is a hard saying, who can accept it'" (Jn 6:51-60).

We reviewed in the chapter on "Greek Heritage," the dissensions which divided the Church and created various camps: Arianism, Nestorianism, Monophysitism, and Monothelitism.

Since there were differences from the beginning of Christianity we should not be surprised that dissension within the Church has continued throughout the centuries. The Eucharist is a means to unity but it must be received with open hearts for unity to take place. There has to be a free will desire for Eucharistic unity.

For people to break bread at the same table of the Lord, the Eucharist should not be held hostage to unreasonable preconditions. Our goal, within the context of Church procedure, should be to return to the spirit of the early Church which allowed all the baptized who believed in the Real Presence and were without serious sin, to share in the breaking of bread together. Then we will emulate that Christian hospitality which Christ gave us as an example. Pope Benedict XVI believes that we should "accept the question of intercommunion with appropriate humility and patience... humbly waiting for God to grant this unity himself. Instead of conducting experiments in this area and robbing the mystery of its greatness and degrading it to an instrument in our hands, we too should learn to celebrate a Eucharist of longing and yearning and in shared prayer and shared hope to walk together with the Lord toward new ways of finding unity" (Ratzinger, 54, 55).

There is a balance needed here. The Western Church recognizes the validity of the sacrament in the Oriental Churches which stem from the apostles. Indeed, an argument can be made that the Eucharist was first celebrated in the East and made its way to the West. It was human action that caused the division. While we must certainly pray and yearn for a return to "breaking bread" together again at the same table of the Lord, we are also given free will by our Lord to take whatever bold actions are necessary to make up for our past mistakes and to restore that unity. In this regard, the West and East can only make progress with the other's acquiescence. Indeed, there should be longing, yearning, prayer and perseverance that after a thousand years of separation East and West would again "break bread" together.

In his homily at the closing Mass of the 24th Italian National Eucharistic Congress in Bari on Sunday, May 29, 2005, Pope Benedict XVI committed himself to working with all his energies to restoring sacramental unity between these two Churches:

> The Eucharist, let us repeat, is the sacrament of unity. But, unfortunately, Christians are divided precisely over the sacrament of unity. All the more reason, therefore, that supported by the Eucharist, we must

feel stimulated to tend with all our strength toward that full unity that Christ ardently desired. Precisely here, in Bari, the city that keeps the bones of St. Nicholas, land of meeting and dialogue with Christian brothers of the East, I would like to confirm my wish to assume a fundamental commitment to work with all my energies in the reconstitution of the full and visible unity of all the followers of Christ. (*L'Osservatore Romano*, N. 22 (1896), 1 June 2005; also *Reign of the Sacred Heart*, 6, 7)

As indicated, in the early centuries there was a gradual movement from home liturgies to church liturgies with the liturgy becoming more formalized. The increasing number of Christians precluded celebrations in smaller homes with movement to larger homes and eventually into church buildings. The problem of feeding so many people also contributed to the separation of the agape meal from the Eucharistic celebration. The non-baptized were required to leave before the Eucharistic celebration.

During the early Middle Ages the West began to describe the real presence of Jesus in the Eucharist by using the term "transubstantiation." This contributed to the differences between Eastern Orthodox and Roman Catholics. The basic statement on transubstantiation was made by the Council of Trent which said that:

Moreover, since Christ our savior said that what he offered under the species of bread was truly his body (Mt 26:26; Mk 14:22; Lk 22:19; 1 Cor 11:24) for this reason it has always been held in the Church of God and this holy synod now declares it once again: through the consecration of the bread and wine there occurs a change (conversio) of the entire substance of bread into the substance of the body of Christ our Lord, and the entire substance of wine into the substance of his blood. This conversion (conversio) has been aptly and properly called by the holy Catholic Church transubstantiation. (Osborne, '87, 194)

Many have tried to explain the presence of Jesus in the Eucharist and what happens to the elements of bread and wine. Thomas Aquinas said that the essence of bread and wine were changed into the matter and form of Christ's body and blood. There is no discernible change in the outward properties (or "accidents" in his terminology) of bread and wine. The elements were no longer bread and wine in a true sense. They continue to exist as material signs of what they had become. The Church says that the elements are not bread and wine despite their appearances. Jesus is physically present in His body and blood.

Jesus is fully present in each host and in each part of each host present in ciboria throughout the world. In the Eucharist, Christ is truly contained. It is the same body that is in heaven, only the manner of presence differs from that which is in heaven. The Church has not definitively explained how the bread and wine and the presence of Jesus both in heaven and in the elements are interrelated. What takes place at the Mass in the consecration of the bread and wine into the reality of the risen Christ remains a mystery (J.T. O'Connor, 281-287).

The problem that the Eastern Orthodox Churches have is that the word "transubstantiation" begins to philosophically define what happens to the bread and wine, something unknown to the early Church. The position in the East is that what happens to the Eucharist is a mystery beyond comprehension and should be accepted by faith.

The Western Church also believes that the Eucharist is a

mystery beyond human understanding. It believes that the Eucharistic mystery transcends human reason and there is no rational explanation of it. Seeking to comprehend one of the sublime truths of the Christian religion through logical processes by theologians is not possible.

The Western Church was pressed to define how the transformation takes place by the Protestant Reformers who claimed that the bread and wine were merely symbolic. Trent used the word "transubstantiation" as a means of defining the "real presence" in human language. Trent did not elaborate on its definition and as a result many have tried to define what Trent meant. Words often take on different meanings, and when those words concern attempts to define a mystery disputes are bound to occur.


EAST IS EAST AND WEST IS WEST.
SHALL THE TWAIN EVER BE TOGETHER AGAIN?

In order to understand the historical development of the Eucharistic experience between the East and the West let us trace briefly the political, cultural and theological factors that contributed to the separation of these Churches. For a thousand years the Christian Church was one. The background for the differences included a changing political scene, cultural differences, Church practices, and a lack of committed leadership. The Roman Empire was in decay while Byzantine political and cultural influence reached its peak in the tenth and eleventh centuries. Further, the period preceding the formal schism, from 867 to 1049, was the low point in the history of the papacy and not conducive to binding differences between East and West. It was not until Leo IX (1049-54) that the papacy found a man who could face its problems with courage, learning, integrity, and a piety needed to restore the papacy.

In addition to a number of theological differences, the patriarchates of the Eastern Church had long been subordinate to the Hellenic emperors, and these would not, until 871, abandon their claim to sovereignty over Rome and its popes. The patriarchs occasionally criticized, disobeyed, and even denounced the emperors; but they were appointed and deposed by the emperors, who called ecclesiastical councils, regulated Church affairs by state law, and published their theological opinions and directives to the ecclesiastical world. The checks on the religious autocracy of the emperor in Eastern Christendom were the power of the monks, the tongue of the patriarch, and the vow taken by the emperor at his coronation by the patriarch, that he would introduce no novelty into the Church.

Differences of language, liturgy, and doctrine drove Latin and Eastern Christianity further and further apart. Hellenic liturgy, ecclesiastical vestments, vessels, and ornaments were more complex, ornate and artistically wrought than those of the West; the Hellenes used leavened bread, the Latins unleavened bread in the Eucharist; the Hellenes prayed standing, the Latins kneeling; the Hellenes baptized by immersion, the Latins by aspersion; Hellenic priests were allowed to marry (prior to their ordination), Latin priests eventually were not; Hellenic priests had beards, Latin priests shaved.

The breakup of the Roman Empire, which had provided political unity, and the lack of adequate communication between East and West, contributed to the differences between East and West. The Trullan Synod of 692 in the East reiterated the privileges of the Patriarch of Constantinople, condemned compulsory celibacy of the clergy, which was developing in the West, and fasting on the Sabbath. Emperors were being crowned and ecclesiastically enthroned in the West curtailing the authority of the Byzantine emperors and the Crusades came to the East and attempted to establish the jurisdiction and canonical authority of the Pope on the Eastern Church. A rift was also caused in 867 when Pope Nicholas I became involved in the election of the Patriarch of Constantinople and tried to ecclesiastically annex Bulgaria.

The official schism occurred in 1054. Cardinal Humbert was sent as the head of a delegation by the West, but rather than come as mediator he delivered demanding letters, did not follow protocol, and published an attack against the Eastern Church calling it a "lair of heretics and heresies." Because of this, Patriarch Michael Cerularios, who was strong minded in his own right, would have nothing to do with him. Frustrated, Humbert, just before the liturgy began at the Cathedral of St. Sophia, marched down the aisle and threw a bull of excommunication on the altar and marched out. A deacon of St. Sophia ran after him begging him to take it back. He refused and the bull was blown away by the wind. Cerularios issued anathemas against the Western Church and published an encyclical explaining the position of the Eastern Church.

Until the time of John XXIII and Patriarch Athenagoras I relations between East and West were almost non-existent. In 1952 the Ecumenical Patriarch Athenagoras, for the first time in one thousand years, visited the Papal representative in Constantinople and he returned the visit. The Patriarch and the Pope exchanged formal letters on Christmas 1958 calling for peace among the Christian Churches. When Paul VI became pope in 1963 a regular correspondence between the two Churches was initiated. Athenagoras and Paul VI met in the Holy Land in January 1964. They embraced and prayed together issuing a joint statement indicating their focus on Jesus Christ, the source of unity and peace. On December 7, 1965, the mutual anathemas pronounced in 1054 by Cardinal Humbert and Patriarch Cerularios were lifted. The Pope and the Patriarch, in their joint statement, expressed regret for the mutual lack of understanding and communication which finally led to the complete cessation of ecclesiastical communion.

Following the lifting of the anathemas, Patriarch Athenagoras visited the Vatican and prayed with Pope Paul VI, and the Pope visited and prayed with the Ecumenical Patriarch in his seat at Constantinople (Istanbul). In the United States Orthodox and Catholic theologians established the "Orthodox-Catholic Consultation." The Consultation has been functioning ever since and is referred to below in the discussion on the filioque.

Pope John Paul II continued his predecessor's efforts toward unity with the Eastern Church. Ecumenical Patriarch Bartholomew referred to this in his statement upon the passing of the Pope into eternal life: "Pope John Paul II envisioned the restoration of the unity of the Christians and he worked for its realization. Thus, and in order to give the mark of his papacy, he visited the Ecumenical Patriarch only a year after his election, and together with (Ecumenical) Patriarch Demetrios declared the formation of the Joint Committee for the inception of the Theological Dialogue between Orthodox and Roman Catholics" (*Orthodox Observer*, March 15-April 15, 2005). One of John Paul II's gestures, which will long be remembered in the East, is the return of the relics of Saints John Chrysostom and Gregory of Nazianzus. The relics were taken by the Crusaders when they sacked Constantinople in 1204. Pope John Paul II has asked forgiveness of the Roman Catholic Church for the actions of the Fourth Crusade. Ecumenical Patriarch Bartholomew, who requested the return of the relics, traveled to Rome to personally receive the relics on November 26, 2004. The relics now rest at the Ecumenical Patriarchate in Constantinople.

## PAPAL PRIMACY AND THEOLOGICAL ISSUES

Pope John Paul II's and Benedict XVI's great desire for unity between East and West, and the sharing of the sacrament of the Eucharist between Eastern Orthodoxy and Roman Catholicism, will probably make little headway until progress is made on the basic theological issues of:

1. The infallibility of and the jurisdictional authority of the Pope.
2. The filioque — that the Holy Spirit is generated both from the Father and the Son.
3. The Doctrine of the Immaculate Conception.
4. The Doctrine of the Assumption of Mary.

### Papal Infallibility and Jurisdiction

With regard to papal infallibility, the Orthodox developed a system which stresses the equality of all bishops. Every diocesan bishop has the right to attend a General Council, to speak and to cast his vote. The bishop of major cities is called "Patriarch" with the Patriarch in Constantinople (Istanbul), currently Bartholomew I, as the head of Orthodoxy. He does not have authoritarian power but rather operates under a conciliar concept of Church administration.

There are 14 autocephalous (independent) Orthodox Churches throughout the world. These Churches appoint their own bishops and administer their own affairs. The Ecumenical Patriarch holds the "primacy of honor" among the bishops of the 14 independent Churches. While he is recognized as the first bishop of the Orthodox Church he does not have jurisdiction over any autocephalous canonical bishop. He has the responsibility for mediating disputes, advocating greater unity among various autocephalous Churches, and for taking the initiative in identifying issues and concerns which must be addressed by the entire Orthodox Church. He also has the responsibility of granting autocephalous status to particular Churches.

Autocephalous Churches include the ancient Churches of Constantinople, Alexandria, Antioch, Jerusalem, Russia and Cyprus, as well as Greece-1850, Serbia-1879, Romania-1885, Poland-1924, Albania-1937, Bulgaria-1945, Georgia-1950 and Czech Republic/Slovakia-1998. The Orthodox Churches in the United States, Australia, South America, Africa and other parts of the world which do not have autocephalous status come under the jurisdiction of the Ecumenical Patriarch.

There are joint annual celebrations in Rome and Istanbul (Constantinople) on the feasts of Sts. Peter and Paul and St. Andrew. On the feast of Sts. Peter and Paul (June 29, 2004 in Rome), John Paul II in addressing Bartholomew said, "We are praying that the Lord of History purifies our memories of every prejudice and resentment and allows us to freely proceed on the road of unity" (*The National Herald*, July 3-4, 2004).

The Orthodox believe that among the patriarchs a special place belongs to the Bishop of Rome, a primacy of honor, with the right under certain conditions to hear appeals from all parts of Christendom. Orthodoxy does not, however, accept the doctrine of papal authority. Orthodox believe that the Pope is the bishop who presides in love and that the Western Church's mistake was to turn the primacy of love into one of supremacy of external power and jurisdiction. John Paul II's great desire for the unity of the Churches of East and West led him to invite contributions on the nature and powers of the papacy, and there have been a number of learned responses both by Catholics and non-Catholics.

## The Filioque

With regard to the filioque, the Western credal statement that the Holy Spirit proceeds from the Father *and* the Son, the Orthodox believe that the Holy Spirit proceeds from the Father *through* the Son. A review of the Christian Scriptures on this question reveals that the Gospel of John is most relevant. The Synoptic Gospels do not treat this question.

In John's Gospel we find several references to the sending of the Advocate, the Paraclete as the Holy Spirit. In Chapter 14, "If you love Me you will keep My commandments. And I will ask the Father, and He will give you another Advocate to be with you always, the Spirit of truth" (Jn 14:15-17a). This is clearly a sending forth of the Spirit by the Father at Jesus' request. In Chapter 16: "But I tell you the truth, it is better for you that I go. For if I do not go, the Advocate will not come to you. But if I go I will send Him to you" (16:7). This is clearly a sending forth of the Spirit by Jesus. Further in the same chapter, "But when He comes, the Spirit of truth, He will guide you to all truth. He will not speak on His own, but He will speak what He hears, and will declare to you the things that are coming. He will glorify Me, because He will take what is Mine and declare it to you. Everything that the Father has is Mine; for this reason I told you that He will take what is Mine and declare it to you" (16:13-15). After Jesus' resurrection He appeared to His disciples and "He breathed on them and said to them, 'Receive the Holy Spirit'" (Jn 20:22). Taken at face value, John's Gospel indicates that before His resurrection (Jn 14:15-17; 14:26) Jesus asks the Father to send the Holy Spirit, while after the resurrection (16:7; 20:22) Jesus himself directs the Holy Spirit.

In the Acts of the Apostles we find, "Exalted at the right hand of God, He received the promise of the Holy Spirit from the Father and poured it forth, as you both see and hear" (2:33).

This is a clear indication that the Father pours forth the Spirit into the Son and through the Son to others. Further, "We are witnesses of these things, as is the Holy Spirit that God has given to those who obey Him" (5:32). The Father gives the Holy Spirit to the Son as well as to those who obey Him. And again, "...how God anointed Jesus of Nazareth with the Holy Spirit and power" (10:38). With regard to the Gentiles, "And God, who knows the heart, bore witness by granting them the Holy Spirit just as He did us" (15:8). There is also the suggestion that the Holy Spirit emanates on His own, "Keep watch over yourselves and over the whole flock of which the Holy Spirit has appointed you overseers, in which you tend the Church of God that He acquired with His own blood" (20:28).

In the Letter to the Romans, Paul writes, "May the God of hope fill you with all joy and peace in believing, so that you may abound in hope by the power of the Holy Spirit" (15:13).

In Hebrews we find, "God added His testimony by signs, wonders, various acts of power, and distribution of the gifts of the Holy Spirit according to His will" (2:4).

The Nicene Creed issued from the Council of Nicea (325) and the further development of the Creed at Constantinople I (381) and succeeding Ecumenical Councils did not have the filioque. For 264 years, after the Council at Nicea, all Christendom recited the Creed which stated that the Holy Spirit proceeded from the Father.

In 589 a Spanish Church Council at Toledo changed the Creed to read that the Holy Spirit proceeded from the Father and the Son and this Creed was adopted by the Spanish Church. From there it spread to France and Germany where it was welcomed by Charlemagne, more for political than for theological reasons. He wanted to get back at the East which did not support his crowning as emperor. Pope Leo III wrote Charlemagne that while he considered the filioque doctrinally sound, he thought it would be a mistake to tamper with the Creed. For hundreds of years the popes patiently did not make an issue of this, but the filioque was finally adopted by Rome at the coronation of Emperor Henry II in Rome in 1014, fifty years before the official separation of the Churches of East and West.

Patriarch Michael Anchialos (1170-1177) wrote that the Pope's primacy remained as long as he professed the true faith, and that he lost that primacy when he adopted the heresy of the filioque. Others have said that if he expressed the same true faith his privileges would be returned.

It is interesting to note that Pope John Paul II in joint ceremonies with Orthodox recited the Creed without the filioque, that is that "the Holy Spirit proceeds from the Father." The North American Orthodox-Catholic Theological Consultation, which consists of Orthodox and Catholic theologians, issued its study on the filioque on October 25, 2003. It focused its discussions on this issue from 1999 to 2003. It recommended "that the Catholic Church as a consequence of the normative and irrevocable dogmatic value of the Creed of 381, use the original Greek text alone in making translations of that Creed for catechetical and liturgical use." No official Church action has thus far been taken. The Orthodox believe that changes in basic dogma should be decided at ecumenical councils at which both East and West participate.

## The Immaculate Conception

With regard to the dogma of the Immaculate Conception, Orthodox believe that it is not so much erroneous as it is superfluous. This has to do with a difference in the interpretation of how original sin is transmitted. The Orthodox tradition agrees that Adam and Eve's original sin affects the human race and has consequences both on the physical and the moral level. It not only results in sickness and physical death but in the weakening of free will and the use of reason. However, it does not believe that it should be interpreted in juridical or quasi-biological terms, as if it were some physical taint of guilt, transmitted through sexual intercourse. This is typically presented as the Augustinian view and is unacceptable to the Orthodox.

The Orthodox belief is that rather than transmission through sexual intercourse, original sin means that human beings are born into an environment where it is easy to do evil and hard to do good. They are conditioned by the accumulated wrong doing and wrong thinking of the human race to which each adds his own deliberate acts of sin. Since we are so interdependent, any action by one member affects the rest. Original sin then is not inherited guilt as envisaged by Augustine. There is, therefore, no need for the dogma, as defined by the Roman Catholic Church that Mary from the first moment of her conception was exempt from original sin and from that point of view is immaculate.

Orthodoxy in its liturgical worship addresses the Theotokos as "spotless" (achrantos), "all holy" (Panaghia), "altogether without stain" (panamonos) (Ware, *The Orthodox Way*, 102). "Never by a single thought did the Mother of God sin, nor did she ever lose grace…" (Ware, *Mary Theotokos*, 11). Mary's title (Panaghia) "all holy" is used in referring to her in typical conversation. For example, in saying "goodbye" a person would say, "the all holy one (Panaghia) be with you." This title is understood to mean that Mary is free from all actual sin, although she was born subject to the effects of original sin. "Thus the Orthodox Church sees in her the supreme fulfillment of sanctity in a human person — the model and paradigm of what it means, by God's grace to be authentically human" (Ware, *Mary Theotokos*, 4). Orthodox join with St. Ephrem, the deacon Syrian saint, and say, "For there is no blemish in thee, my Lord, and no stain in thy Mother" (Ware, *The Orthodox Way*, 103).

## The Assumption

The dogma of the Assumption causes the least of differences between East and West. Orthodox refer to the death of the Mother of God as the "dormition" of Mary. The Assumption is clearly affirmed in Orthodox worship but it is not declared dogma. While not explicitly spelled out in dogma, as in the Roman Catholic Church, Orthodox believe that after her death Mary was assumed into heaven where she dwells with her body as well as her soul in eternal glory with her Son. It is not only Mary's unique privilege, but also an anticipation of that which is the hope of all humanity (Ware, *Mary Theotokos*, 16).

Of the four issues discussed above that impede intercommunion between East and West, the most serious to the Orthodox is the infallibility and jurisdiction of the Pope. To the Orthodox, dogmas produced by the Church must be debated and passed in ecumenical councils where, as indicated above, both East and West participate and each bishop has the right to participate and vote. The dogma cannot be unilaterally proclaimed by the Pope without ecumenical council consideration, say the Orthodox.

With regard to unity between East and West, Vatican II's *Decree on Ecumenism* states that "in order to restore community and unity or preserve them, one must 'impose no burden beyond what is indispensable' (Ac 15:28)" (III, I, 18). This is a phrase often repeated by the Roman pontiff in his desire for unity with the East.


## INTERCOMMUNION

"On Admitting Other Christians to Eucharistic Communion in the Catholic Church," Vatican II says:

The Ecumenical Directory gives different directions for the admission to Holy Communion of separated Eastern Christians and of others. The reason is that the Eastern Churches, though separated from us, have true sacraments, above all because of the apostolic succession, the priesthood, and the Eucharist, which unite them to us by close ties, so that the risk of obscuring the relation between Eucharistic communion and ecclesial communion is somewhat reduced. Recently the Holy Father recalled that: "between our Church and the venerable Orthodox Churches there exists already an almost total communion, though it is not yet perfect: it results from our joint participation in the mystery of Christ and of His Church." (V)

In his encyclical *Ecclesia De Eucharistia* Pope John Paul II repeated Vatican II's prohibition of concelebrating the same Eucharistic liturgy until there is "full communion in the bonds of the profession of faith, the sacraments and ecclesial governance" (44). However, he also said, "the same is not true with respect to the administration of the Eucharist *under special circumstances to individual persons* belonging to Churches or Ecclesial Communities not in full communion with the Catholic Church. In this case, in fact, the intention is to meet a grave spiritual need … not to bring about *intercommunion*.… This was the approach taken by the Second Vatican Council when it gave guidelines for responding to Eastern Christians separated in good faith from the Catholic Church, who spontaneously ask to receive the Eucharist from a Catholic minister and are properly disposed…." (45).

Vatican II covers both Eastern Christians seeking the sacraments from a Catholic minister and also Catholics seeking the sacraments from non-Catholic ministers with valid sacraments:

Eastern Christians who are separated in good faith from the Catholic Church, if they are rightly disposed and make such request of their own accord, may be given the Sacraments of Penance, the Eucharist and the Anointing of the Sick. Catholics also may ask for those same sacraments from non-Catholic ministers in whose Church there are valid sacraments, as often as necessary or true spiritual benefit recommends such action, and access to a Catholic priest is physically or morally impossible. (*Decree on the Catholic Eastern Churches*, 27)

Canon Law incorporates the Vatican II pronouncement:

Code of Canon Law 844.3. Catholic ministers may licitly administer the sacraments of penance, Eucharist and anointing of the sick to members of the oriental Churches which do not have full communion with the Catholic Church, if they ask on their own for the sacraments and are properly disposed. This holds also for members of other Churches, which in the judgment of the Apostolic See are in the same condition as the oriental Churches as far as these sacraments are concerned.

While there is a legal basis for it from the Roman Catholic Church, in actual practice very little intercommunion takes place. If for example, an Orthodox attends a Roman Catholic Mass, say for a funeral or a wedding, he or she is asked by the Orthodox Church not to receive Holy Communion. If for example, a Roman Catholic attends an Orthodox liturgical service and because of such attendance cannot attend a Catholic Mass, he or she has met their Sunday obligation. However, the Orthodox

Church allows Holy Communion only for its members. Where there is an emergency situation and a Catholic minister is asked to assist an Orthodox person, and there is no Orthodox minister available, he would be required by charity and allowed by law to administer the sacrament(s).

## PREPARATION FOR AND FREQUENCY
## OF HOLY COMMUNION

### Fasting

Fasting is common in the Hebrew Scriptures and Christianity being born out of a Jewish context also practices fasting preceding important feasts and events. Moses fasted forty days on Mt. Sinai and came down with the Ten Commandments (Ex 34:28). Elijah fasted forty days as he sought God's will (1 K 19:8). David fasted after Nathan, the prophet, pointed out his sins of adultery with Bathsheba and the murder of her husband Uriah (2 S 12:16-17). Ahab, urged by his wife Jezebel, did evil and was warned by Elijah of the forthcoming punishment of the Lord. Ahab put on sackcloth and the Lord delayed his punishment (1 K 21:27-29). There are numerous other examples of fasting in the Jewish Scriptures (Ezk 8:23; Ba 1:5; Ne 1:4; Jdt 4:13; Est 4:16; Jr 36:6, 9; and Jl 1:14, 2:15).

In the Christian Scriptures our Lord fasted forty days after His baptism and prior to the beginning of His public ministry (Mt 4:2; Mk 1:12; Lk 4:2). Jesus also gave instructions on how to fast to His disciples (Mt 6:16, 17). Anna, the prophetess, was constantly in the Temple in fasting and prayer (Lk 2:37).

In a direct reference to the liturgy, we find that in the church in Antioch "while they were engaged in the liturgy of the Lord and were fasting, the Holy Spirit spoke to them" (Ac 13:2). Paul and Barnabas on their first mission, installed presbyters in each church, "and with prayer and fasting, commended them to the Lord" (Ac 14:23). In his Second Letter to the Corinthians, Paul writes that he had to undergo many hardships including "beatings, imprisonments and riots; as men familiar with hard work, sleepless nights and fastings" (2 Cor 6:5).

Joachim Jeremias believes that Jesus fasted at the Passover supper. He points out that Jesus refrained from eating the bread and drinking the cup until the coming of the kingdom of God (Lk 22:16, 18).

The custom of fasting before receiving the Eucharist became prevalent in the Church after the third century. As fasting became the practice, more people stayed away from Holy Communion. Easter was preceded by a forty day fast emulating Jesus' forty day fast in the desert. This was also a time of religious instruction, recollection and meditation. In the Eastern Church, fasting during the forty days plus, meant that no meat, fowl or fish were eaten and no wine or hard drink taken. Many abstained from oil as well as all cooked food and lived on bread and water.

## Frequency of Receiving Holy Communion

Not everyone was enthusiastic with such austerity. They felt shamed in comparison to their more austere neighbors and did not attend Church services. St. John Chrysostom would urge the people to attend. He stressed that fasting was not more important than listening to the word of God and receiving Him in Holy Communion. The Church went from a practice of receiving communion every time the assembly met to one of infrequent communion by the fourth century. As bishop of Constantinople, Chrysostom complained that while there was a daily oblation there was no one present to communicate.

The same trend occurred in the West. As the situation

worsened it became necessary to require Holy Communion on Sundays and holy days (Capitulary of Charlemagne, V.I, No. 82). The Council of Tours in the ninth century required that Christians should communicate on Christmas Day, Easter Sunday and Pentecost. The Lateran Council held that all the faithful should confess their sins at least once a year and receive communion during Easter. The Council of Trent said the faithful should not only communicate once a year but every time they assisted at Mass if their consciences were "pure and guiltless" before God.

In the latter part of the nineteenth century, practicing Roman Catholics generally communicated on the first Sunday of each month and on major feast days. Pious Roman Catholics communicated once a week and the fervent as many as three times a week.

In the Eastern Church Holy Communion was received less frequently than in the West. Part of the reason for this was the more than four hundred year Turkish occupation of Hellas extending to the twentieth century for some parts of the country. The Turks did not allow any seminaries, few priests were educated and their knowledge of theology was limited. The idea of unworthiness persisted resulting in the infrequent reception of the Eucharist.

The place where Holy Communion was received was related to the frequency of communion. Both Tertullian (*Ad uxorem* 1:25) and St. Cyprian (*De lapsis*, 26) indicated the faithful in times of persecution took a supply of the Eucharistic bread to their homes so that they might communicate daily. St. Basil in a letter written in 372 stated that people in the desert or in remote localities had communion at home. In Syria the practice of keeping communion at home was prevalent as late as the sixth century.

The practice of receiving Holy Communion regularly through the third century began to decline because of an exaggerated humility regarding the Eucharist. In the West many monks taught that the recipient must not only be free of mortal sin but must also lead a perfect life conformed to Christ or the sacrament would cause harm. In the East, the feeling of unworthiness had the result of primarily reserving communion for Easter. This practice spread West as far as Milan.

From the sixth to the thirteenth centuries there was a general decline in the frequent reception of the Eucharist. Clement of Alexandria and St. Jerome taught that married couples should refrain from sexual relations on the days they receive Holy Communion. This teaching lasted through the Middle Ages when St. Bede taught that married couples could receive communion weekly with the young and the old if they practiced continence and reflected chastity in their lives.

The Jansenistic heresy, which taught that humans were sinful and unworthy to receive the Eucharist, was fought by St. Alphonsus Maria de Liguori in the eighteenth century who wrote favoring frequent communion, leaving the frequency of receiving communion to one's confessor.

During the nineteenth century, Eucharistic congresses, forty hour devotions and perpetual adoration developed primarily because Holy Communion could be received only infrequently. In 1905, Pope Pius X issued a decree on frequent communion stating that the recipient must be in a state of grace for daily communion, have a right intention, be free of deliberate venial sin, and make a fitting preparation and thanksgiving.

In the Orthodox Church the trend from the fifth century on was one of infrequent Holy Communion because of a sense of unworthiness and the necessary austerities practiced before communion.

## Current Practices in Receiving Holy Communion

The frequency of receiving the Eucharist was roughly similar in both the Eastern and Western Churches except for recent history. Both East and West began by celebrating and receiving the Eucharist daily. Later, the weekly assembly was the common practice with baptized participants receiving the Eucharist at each of the celebrations of the "breaking of the bread."

As we have seen in the beginning there was a meal eaten prior to the reception of the Eucharist. Those who were not baptized partook of the meal and were excused prior to the Eucharistic celebration. The "Our Father," was to be said only by the baptized. The words were sacred and not to be prayed by the nonbaptized. Even reference to the Eucharist was kept secret and mysterious. This was probably due partly because of fear of persecution but primarily as a sign of reverence for a great mystery reserved for the initiated who understood its significance. Early references in the *Didache*, for example, were veiled concerning the Holy Eucharist.

East and West both began to commune infrequently primarily because of a growing sense of unworthiness which stemmed from and was supported by the heresies of Arianism and Jansenism. The clergy varied on this matter and at times tried to get the faithful to commune more often and at other times taught strict pre-conditions of purity and "state of grace" requirements.

In recent history, receiving the Holy Eucharist frequently has become the mark of the Roman Catholic Church. There is a growing trend by Orthodox to commune more frequently. In some parishes, where the pastor has aggressively encouraged frequent communion, there is weekly reception of the Eucharist by many of the faithful.

## Eligibility to Receive Holy Communion

Jesus said to the Pharisee who had invited Him, "Whenever you give a lunch or dinner, do not invite your friends or brothers or relatives or wealthy neighbors. They might invite you in return and thus repay you. No, when you have a reception, invite beggars and the crippled, the lame and the blind" (Lk 14:12-13).

The Lord's table is open to everyone. Assemblies of Christians who "do this in remembrance of Me" are not to be restrictive in terms of race, economic or social class. Jesus does not want His Church to turn into an exclusive club. Within the Church He does not want divisive cliques. He taught that the crippled, the beggar, the poor and the lame must sit side by side with the wealthy and prominent as equals.

Sinners are also invited to the Lord's table. The Pharisees and scribes complained against the Lord, "This man welcomes sinners and eats with them" (Lk 15:2). Jesus answered the Pharisees and scribes by citing the parables of the lost sheep and the woman who lost a silver piece and how happy the shepherd and the woman were when they found what they had lost (Lk 15:4-10).

Benedict XVI, while a cardinal, said this should be interpreted as an invitation, by Jesus, to reconciliation rather than an automatic invitation to the Eucharistic table. The Eucharist, he says, is "the sacrament of those who have let themselves be reconciled by God, who have become members of His family and put themselves into His hands" (Ratzinger, 61). He quotes the *Didache* (10.6) in support of his argument, that the "priest" before distributing the Eucharist says, "If anyone is holy, let him come. If not let him repent." Benedict's principle is followed by both the Orthodox and Catholic Churches, both of which do not automatically allow anyone to the Eucharistic table. The

Churches of the East and West recognize that all are sinners and are invited to the table of reconciliation, and after being reconciled, and becoming members of the family, they may also sit at the table of the Holy Eucharist.

In the Orthodox Church a person is eligible for Holy Communion if he/she is:

1. Orthodox — A person may not legally receive Holy Communion unless he or she is a member of the Orthodox Church.
2. The Orthodox member must be in good standing.

For example, if a person is married in a church, other than the Orthodox Church, that person is not in good standing. If a person is civilly divorced, he or she may not receive the Eucharist until such time as the Church grants its decree of divorce. The Church grants a divorce for adultery but no person is granted a divorce more than three times.

3. The Orthodox receives Holy Communion from the moment he or she is baptized and confirmed, all the sacraments being given at the same time by the priest.

In the Roman Catholic Church, those eligible for Holy Communion are:

1. Any baptized person who is not prohibited by law.

While the faithful may licitly receive Holy Communion only from Roman Catholic ministers, when necessity requires or genuine spiritual advantage suggests, it is lawful for the faithful for whom it is physically or morally impossible to approach a Roman Catholic minister, to receive the Eucharist from non-Roman Catholic ministers in whose Churches those sacraments are valid.

2. Children who have reached the age of reason, who are cor-

rectly prepared and who precede communion by sacramental confession, may receive communion.

3. Those who are excommunicated or interdicted and who obstinately persist in grave sin are not to be admitted to Holy Communion. Similarly, a person who is conscious of a grave sin is not eligible to celebrate Mass or receive Holy Communion without prior sacramental confession (Code of Canon Law, Nos. 844, 912, 914, 915, 916).

## Holy Communion for Children

As noted above the Orthodox Church baptizes, chrismates (confirms) and gives Holy Communion to infants all at the same time, differing from the Roman Catholic Church which reserves communion and confirmation to a later date. In the early days of Christianity children were baptized with their families. Entire families were baptized together. The first century Christian document, the *Didache*, indicates that only the baptized were allowed to receive Holy Communion. While children are not specifically mentioned, it could be assumed that if they were baptized they would also be eligible for communion. There is no mention of exclusion for children.

Orthodox believe that if Holy Communion is withheld from baptized infants and children but given to baptized adults there would be an exclusivity in membership within the ecclesia. Orthodox believe that one cannot be partly Christian.

St. Cyprian (about 300) attested to the practice of infant communion. St. Augustine (353-430) said that children were receiving the precious blood or both the holy body and precious blood.

Infant communion was practiced in the Roman Catholic Church until the thirteenth century. The vestiges of Arianism contributed to infrequent Holy Communion and prevented children from receiving it until they reached the age of reason and had Christian instruction. The Lateran Council (1215), by requiring that all persons reaching the age of reason receive the Sacraments of Penance and the Eucharist at least once a year, approved this practice. The heresy of Jansenism further restricted receiving communion by all, including children, because it regarded the reception of the Eucharist as a reward for virtue. Pius X decreed that children should be admitted to communion as soon as they could distinguish between the "bread of life" and ordinary bread.

There is much we do not know of the intellectual and spiritual perception of infants and children. Orthodox would argue that not only should there not be two classes of the baptized but that children who grow and become accustomed to receiving the Eucharist naturally, can be taught as early as possible what they are consuming.

Bishop Kallistos Ware summarizes the Orthodox view:

In the Orthodox Church communion is given to infants from the moment of their Baptism onwards. This means that the earliest childhood memories of the Church that an Orthodox Christian has will probably be linked with coming up to receive Christ's Body and Blood; and the last conscious action of his life, he hopes, will also be the reception of the divine Gifts. So his experience of Holy Communion extends over the whole range of his conscious life. (Ware, *The Orthodox Way*, 145, 146)

The effect of the Eucharist on the innocent souls of infants and children is a mystery. Jesus said, "Let the children come to Me. Do not hinder them. The kingdom of God belongs to such as these" (Mt 19:14).

## Preparation for Holy Communion

The Orthodox Church believes that whoever approaches the Eucharist must do it with faith, reverence and purity. Confession (Metanoia) is practiced infrequently by Greek Orthodox and it is not the practice to confess one's sins before communion. Russian Orthodox confess more frequently. An Orthodox will pray and fast before receiving the Holy Eucharist. The Orthodox Prayer Book includes prayers written by the Church Fathers designed to be read before and after communion. Following is an excerpt of prayer before communion:

> I am not worthy, Master and Lord, that You should enter under the roof of my soul. Yet in as much as You desire to live in me as the lover of men, I approach with boldness. You have commanded: let the doors be opened which You alone have made and You shall enter with Your love.... You shall enter and enlighten my darkened reasoning. I believe that You will do this. (Coniaris, 137)

The Orthodox Church has not set the number of days for fasting before communion except for certain major feast days, the most important of which is Easter. This normally includes abstaining from meat and any animal derivative such as cheese, milk, eggs, soups or broths from meats and any product which contains such derivatives. It is considered a discipline of the body to partake of Christ's body.

In terms of preparation, we have references in the *Didache* to fasting on Wednesdays and Fridays but the purpose of such fasting is unclear. It is interesting to note that devout Orthodox who are frequent communicants still fast, or at least abstain, on

Wednesdays and Fridays suggesting that this practice has ancient roots.

Fasting prior to major feast days includes the forty plus days prior to Easter. Additional fasts include the period from the Monday following the first Sunday after Pentecost until June 29, the feast of the Holy Apostles; in preparation for the feast of the Virgin Mary from August 1 to August 15; and before Christmas from November 15 to Christmas day.

In contrast, the Roman Catholic Church takes a more liberal approach in its requirements for preparation to receive the Holy Eucharist. An individual who intends to receive Holy Communion is to abstain from food or drink, with the exception of water, for at least one hour before receiving communion (Canon 917). Those who are advanced in age or who suffer from any infirmity, as well as those who take care of them, can receive the Holy Eucharist even if they have eaten something during the previous hour. It is left up to the individual if he or she wishes to fast longer than one hour before receiving the sacrament. Other requirements include fasting and abstinence from meat on Ash Wednesday and Good Friday and abstinence from meat on Fridays during Lent.

While the requirements for preparation to receive Holy Communion have not changed much in the Orthodox Church, the Roman Catholic Church, in order to encourage full participation in the sacrament, has liberalized fasting requirements. The traditional total fast from midnight prescribed in the 1917 Canon Code was reduced to a three hour fast by Pius XII and to a one hour fast in 1964 by Paul VI.

## Frequency of Holy Communion — Current Practice

Based on the preparations alone Roman Catholics would receive communion more frequently than Orthodox. More than stricter preparation is involved here, however, and that, as indicated above, is the underlying traditional belief held by many Orthodox lay persons that one is not worthy to receive the sacrament very often. Most Orthodox who are in sacramental communion with their Church receive communion at least three times a year. Almost all attending receive communion on the holy days of Easter and Christmas.

In contrast, the great majority of Roman Catholics attending Sunday Mass receive Holy Communion. This has become the common practice in recent years and the oddity would be the person who remained in the pew during communion. A person who has received communion may receive it once more on the same day but must participate in the liturgy on both occasions (Canon 917). The Roman Catholic Church requires that the faithful receive communion at least once a year and that this requirement be fulfilled during the Easter season unless it is fulfilled at another time for just cause.

While the two Churches may seem at opposite ends in terms of frequency of communion by their members, there is not that much difference theologically or pastorally. As indicated above, many bishops and priests of the Orthodox Church in the United States urge their faithful to receive communion regularly and there has been a marked increase in the frequency of receiving Holy Communion. Orthodox clergymen are educating their people on the soundness of the early Church practice of receiving communion when the liturgy is celebrated. While it may not be καθ ημεραν (each day) at least it may be καθ εβδομαδα (each week).

In the Roman Catholic Church daily Mass is celebrated and a devout Catholic has the opportunity to receive the Eucharist daily. Vatican II urges parish priests, confessors and preachers to exhort the people to frequent or daily reception of the Blessed Eucharist (*Constitution on the Sacred Liturgy*, I, 37). There is also an extensive use of lay extraordinary ministers of the Eucharist to bring communion to the sick and home bound. In the Orthodox Church the non-monastic clergy do not celebrate the Eucharist each day, only on Sundays and major feast days. Most Orthodox priests are married. One of the requirements for fasting by married priests is that they abstain from sexual relations on the day before the liturgy is celebrated. This effectively eliminates the opportunity for the faithful to receive Holy Communion on a daily basis. The historical basis for this is not clear but it could stem from the practice of married Jewish priests who abstained from sexual relations while on duty in the Temple.

## Body Only or Body and Blood

Holy Communion is always given under both species by the Orthodox Church. It is based on the Lord's Supper when the Lord offered both the bread and the wine to those present. The Orthodox Church does not believe that Roman Catholics are sacramentally correct in offering the body only at the Liturgy of the Eucharist. The Roman Catholic Church believes that one is partaking of the whole of Jesus if any part of either the body or blood is received. The Roman Catholic Church fed its communicants with both the body and blood until the twelfth century.

The problem came to the fore when Viaticum was administered by intinction and was questioned on the basis that unless both body and cup were received one did not truly receive Holy Communion. It turned a practical question into a doctrinal one and forced the Church to look at the practice of communion under one species in a more sympathetic way.

It was the Utraquist controversy that forced the Church to make pronouncements with respect to the presence of Jesus in either the bread or the wine as well as in both. The Utraquists insisted that both species be partaken for a valid Holy Communion. The Eucharistic cup to all the faithful was a practice in the early Church, but by the fourteenth century had fallen into disuse for almost four centuries. Some of the Utraquists also demanded that the Eucharist be celebrated after a meal as was the practice in the early Church and that in order to do this the Church's rules on fasting should be abolished (J.T. O'Connor, 130). At the Council of Trent it was determined that partaking of any part of the body or blood of Christ was a valid communion (DS 1731, 1732). It was also determined that it be left to the Pope to decide when and under what circumstances the offering of the communion cup should be given to those requesting it.

Vatican II encourages Communion under both kinds:

> Holy Communion, considered as a sign, has a fuller meaning when it is received under both kinds. For under this form (leaving intact the principles of the Council of Trent, by which under either species or kind there is received the true sacrament and Christ whole and entire), the sign of the Eucharist appears more perfectly. Moreover, it is more clearly shown how the new and eternal Covenant is ratified in the Blood of the Lord, as it also expresses the relation of the Eucharistic banquet to the eschatological banquet in the Kingdom of the Father (Mt 26:27-29). (*Constitution on the Sacred Liturgy*, I, 32)

Partaking of Holy Communion under both species is increasingly being practiced by the Roman Catholic Church. It allows Holy Communion to be given under the form of bread alone or under both bread and wine. It can also be given under the form of wine alone in case of necessity (Can. 925).

There is general agreement that partaking of both the bread and the cup is more indicative of the Lord' Supper. Jesus offered both the bread and the wine as His body and blood. He asked James and John whether they would be willing to drink of the same cup that He would drink from (Mk 10:38). Drinking from the same cup signifies total commitment to Jesus.

There is a distinction between the liturgical celebration, where both bread and wine are increasingly being used in the Roman Catholic Church, and bringing Holy Communion to the sick. The latter makes it difficult, although not impossible, to give the precious blood as well as the holy body of Christ to the sick. From a practical point of view it is the body of Christ that can more efficiently be given to the sick. There are times when a sick person can only receive a drop or two of the precious blood, as allowed by Canon law.

## Leavened or Unleavened Bread

The Eastern Orthodox Church follows the Johannine Gospel while the Roman Catholic Church follows the Synoptic Gospels with regard to whether the Holy Eucharist was instituted on the Day of Preparation, or the day before. As a result the Eastern Church offers leavened bread while unleavened bread is offered by the Western Church. Both Churches used leavened bread during the first eight centuries when the Western Church began using unleavened bread.

As indicated earlier, part of the confusion lies in the different ways a day is determined. For the Jews the new day began at sundown and ended at sundown the next day, while the West calculates the new day beginning at midnight. The Passover lamb could be slaughtered by the priests on Wednesday and the Lord's Supper celebrated after sundown, which would make it Thursday by Jewish time but still Wednesday by Western time.

The Orthodox Church uses leavened bread based on the fact that the Lord's Supper was celebrated on Thursday the day before the preparation for the Passover. Jesus was brought before Pilate on the Preparation Day for Passover (Jn 19:14) and the crucifixion and death of Jesus took place on the Day of Preparation according to all four Gospels (Mt 27:62; Mk 15:42; Lk 23:54; Jn 19:24).

The Orthodox believe that the Lord's Supper was not on the day of the Passover and unleavened bread would not have been used. The word used in the Bible is αρτος (artos) or leavened bread not αζυμα (azyma) or unleavened bread. Further, it was against the law to crucify anyone during Passover time. If Jesus used unleavened bread it would have been the Passover period.

## Holy Communion Outside the Liturgy

In the Orthodox Church the place to receive Holy Communion is essentially in the church during the celebration of the liturgy. When a church is being established in a community, the assembly could meet in various places, such as a store front, but eventually a church structure, with definitive iconostasis, is established. As indicated, there are no extraordinary ministers of the Eucharist. Only the priest or deacon may bring communion to the sick in hospitals and homes.

In the Catholic Church, acolytes, who are called extraordinary ministers of the Eucharist, as pointed out above, are lay persons active in bringing Holy Communion to the sick. The ordinary minister of Holy Communion is a bishop, priest, or deacon (Can. 910).

In the Catholic Church, unlike the Orthodox Church, the celebration may take place on any day and any hour, except those times excluded by liturgical norms. The celebration is normally celebrated in a sacred place but can take place in a respectable place as necessity demands. For example, this would include hospitals, homes, in the field with troops. It can also be celebrated in another church that does not have full communion with the Catholic Church as long as scandal is avoided.

## Other Forms of Eucharistic Worship

The Western Church has developed forms of Eucharistic worship not common to the Eastern Church. There is, for example, worship of the exposed Eucharist in the Catholic Church. Many also pray before the Eucharist enclosed in the tabernacle. Religious orders such as the Sisters of the Society of the Sacred Hearts of Jesus and Mary and the Blessed Sacrament Order have an emphasis on, and particular devotion to the Eucharist, including devotion to the exposed Eucharist. For more than a hundred years the members of the Arch Confraternity of Nocturnal Adoration have been praying before the exposed Eucharist during the hours of the night.

As pointed out in our review of Scripture, David longed and thirsted for the living God and to gaze on Him in the house of God (Ps 42:1-3, 5); and in Psalm 134, "Lift up your hands toward the sanctuary and bless the Lord" (v. 2).

The original and primary purpose of reserving the Eucharist in the church outside of Mass was to give Viaticum to the dying with secondary purposes being the distribution of the Eucharist outside of Mass and the adoration of Jesus Christ. The Church exhorts the faithful to worship Christ the Lord in the Blessed Sacrament and asks that pastors give the faithful the opportunity to pray before the Holy Eucharist (*Constitution on the Sacred Liturgy*, III, 50, 51).

Also available, but not common, in the Western Church is

spiritual communion. When one desires to receive sacramental communion and it is not possible to receive it corporeally, one may seek communion spiritually. The Council of Trent mentions it twice. The practice appeared in the latter Middle Ages as a substitute for sacramental communion which was rarely received during this period. It was common practice from the twelfth to the fifteenth centuries to gaze on the Sacred Host for the purpose of adoration and to receive the Lord spiritually. The Sacred Host would also be brought to the sick so that they could adore and receive the Lord spiritually. Vatican II mentions it briefly, "When the faithful adore Christ present in the sacrament, they should remember that this presence derives from the sacrifice and is directed towards both sacramental and spiritual communion" (Ibid., III, 50).

The same theological principle applies to spiritual communion as that of baptism of desire. The desire for communion can result in receipt of the spiritual benefits of Holy Communion. The spiritual benefits received are consonant with the disposition of the person desiring the sacrament. A spiritual communion, strictly speaking, does not require one to look at the exposed sacrament.

Spiritual communion is an innovative approach to communing with the Lord, spurred on by the inability to receive Him sacramentally. It is closely connected to adoration and prayer before the exposed Sacred Host or before a tabernacle containing the sacrament. It is primarily unique to the Western Church and reflects the desire of the faithful to commune with Jesus.

St. Alphonsus Maria de Liguori suggested the following prayer formula for spiritual communion: "My Jesus I believe that You are really present in the most Holy Sacrament. I love You above all things, and I desire to possess You within my soul. Since I cannot now receive You sacramentally, come at least spiritually into my heart. (Pause) I embrace You as being already there and unite myself wholly to You. Amen."

St. Thomas Aquinas and St. Alphonsus both taught that spiritual communion produced similar effects as sacramental communion, depending on one's disposition, earnestness with which Jesus is desired and the love with which Jesus is welcomed (Manelli, 50).

# VIII

## COMMUNION TOGETHER -
### Κοινονια Μαζι

O ne of the reasons we find the mystery of the Cross so difficult to understand and accept is that we have a tendency to accept and love those who are like us. We find security and affection in our ethnicity, in those who are of the same cultural, educational and economic class. We are discriminating as to whom we will invite to our house and to our table. Yet these human inclinations are what St. Paul was asking the Corinthians to discard when he criticized the divisions, the selfishness, the greed and the lack of concern for others in their Eucharistic gathering (1 Cor 11:17-33). These are the natural feelings that we must let die in order to live with the Eucharistic Christ. If we do not put to death these inclinations they will impede our ability to love one another and to receive and return God's love to Him.

Paul and the other early evangelists used the word αγαπη (agape) which connotes a selfless love that is given to the beloved without expecting any benefit in return. The true lover, by his/her very nature loves for the sake of loving. This is a Christian love because it imitates the love of Jesus Christ and originates and is sustained by God's eternal love.

Αγαπη (agape), if truly possessed will overcome ethnic, cultural and economic differences. It will also overcome Church rules and decrees which are based on historical differences, which Christian charity demands, not only confession, but forgiveness and reconciliation.

The prayer of Jesus was for one flock. He did not establish many churches but one Church. Both East and West recognize that divisions result from human weakness. It is the Holy Spirit that is guiding the two back together again. There must, however, be the will to accept the prompting of the Holy Spirit.

"Breaking bread" together has not come much closer to reality since Paul VI and Athenagoras I of the Western and Eastern Churches indicated their support for joint Holy Communion. Progress appears ponderously slow. It must be remembered, however, that it took centuries for the two Churches to cease "breaking bread" together and, it may take more time than both would like, to again sit together at the same table. Families do have their disagreements but eventually compassionate leaders come forth who bring them back to a warm embrace and they sit and eat together again.

# IX

## LETTER TO THE CHURCHES
## OF THE EAST AND WEST

To the Churches of God that are in Rome and Constantinople "who have been sanctified in Christ Jesus, called to be holy, with all who call upon the name of our Lord Jesus Christ. Grace and peace to you from God our Father and the Lord Jesus Christ" (1 Cor 1:2, 3).

"I continually thank God for the grace bestowed on you in Christ Jesus, in whom you have been enriched in every way, so that you are not lacking in any spiritual gift. Our Lord Jesus Christ will keep you faithful to the end, irreproachable until the day of our Lord Jesus" (1 Cor 1:4-8).

"I beg you, brethren, in the name of our Savior and Lord that there be no divisions among you" (1 Cor 1:10). "What I have to say to you now is not said in praise. I hear that when you assemble there are divisions among you" (1 Cor 11:17, 18). Those of you from the East go to one house to celebrate the Lord's Supper and those from the West to another. If the Lord Jesus is one with the Father and the Holy Spirit, and His prayer for the Church is that all be one (Jn 17:21), how can you separate and celebrate in this manner? "Shall I praise you for this? In this matter I do not praise you" (1 Cor 11:22). "I urge you brethren, to be alert for those who create dissensions and obstacles, in opposition to the teaching you have learned. Such people do not serve our Lord Jesus Christ" (Rm 16:17, 18).

My fellow Christians of the East and the West, you are the beloved of our Lord Jesus Christ in whom resides the Father's love with the Holy Spirit. You are children of the new Eve, brothers and sisters of Jesus. You are of the family of God, destined for a life in eternal existence with the Holy Trinity. In a little while we shall see each other no more, and, yet in a little while we shall see each other again (cf. Jn 16:16). Do you think the heavenly Church is divided? "Many will come from the East and the West and will recline at table in the kingdom of God" (Mt 8:11; Lk 13:29). Do you think there will be a separate table for those from the East and a separate table for those from the West? Will not our hearts be pure, with no factions or divisions — only αγαπη (agape)?

In the unfathomable mystery of our Creator, He willed that the eternal heaven would merge with earth in a nuptial embrace that begot the God-Man, Jesus Christ. This is no longer merely prefigurement, as in Greek mythology, when the divinity chose to marry a human person and is called a sacred marriage (ιερος γαμος). This was the most sacred of marriages. God chose the purest soil, a dwelling undarkened by sin, a bough in which no blur of either kind had touched this virgin rind, to bring forth His Son. And what of this most holy θεοτοκος (Theotokos) who brought forth the Savior of the world? Does her fertility cease? In the mystery of God is the historical Mary now merely enjoying the eternal bliss, or is she the Life-Giving Fountain of the Theotokos (Η Ζωοδοχος Πηγη) whose fertility brings forth countless children of God?

Our Lord Jesus Christ is with us. He is present in the Holy Eucharist. And where did He get His body and blood with which He feeds us? No other than from the all holy one (Παναγια). She is the mother of the Eucharist as she is the mother of the

God-Man. She is the Theotokos, the instrument of God, who brings Him forth into the world for our salvation.

It is wise to ask for her intercession that we may receive her son, our Lord, our God, our Savior and our Brother, worthily. Since she is the mother of us all in the order of grace, we pray that when we are one with Jesus in Holy Communion we may also be one with each other. Is this not the unity that our Lord, as our high priest, seeks in the mystical family, that He may present us as one holy oblation to God the Father?

With her maternal love, which God pours into her, the Theotokos seeks to gather all her children together as one family of God. We love our Holy Mother so much that we will accede to her wishes, resolve our differences, seek forgiveness from each other and "break bread" together at the same table again.

Παναγια μαζη σας και η χαρις του κυριου Ιησου Χριστου μετα του πνευματος υμον. May the All Holy One be with you and may the grace of the Lord Jesus Christ be with your spirit.

Andrew J. Gerakas

# BIBLIOGRAPHY

## Books

Abbott, W. gen. ed., *The Documents of Vatican II*. New York: America Press, 1966.

*Ancient Christian Writers.* "The Epistles of St. Clement of Rome and St. Ignatius of Antioch." Westminster, MD: The Newman Book Shop, 1946.

*Apostolic Tradition of Hippolytus.* New York: Anchor Books, 1962.

Bellitto, C., *The General Councils.* New York/Mahwah, NJ: Paulist Press, 2002.

Bernier, P.J., ed., *Bread From Heaven.* New York/Ramsey/Toronto: 1977.

Brown, R., *Priest and Bishop.* New York: Paulist Press, 1970.

Calivas, C., *Essays in Theology and Liturgy, Volume Three, Aspects of Orthodox Worship.* Brookline, MA: Holy Cross Orthodox Press, 2003.

*Catechism of the Catholic Church.* Liguori, MO: Liguori Publications, 1994.

Chadwick, H., *The Early Church.* New York: Penguin Books, 1993.

*Code of Canon Law, Latin-English Edition.* Washington, DC: Canon Law Society of America, 1983.

Congar, Y., *Lay People in the Church.* Westminster, MD: Classics, Inc., 1985.

_____. *Power and Poverty in the Church.* Baltimore, MD: Helicon, 1964.

Coniaris, A., *Introducing the Orthodox Church*. Minneapolis, MN: Light and Life Publishing Co., 1982.

Dych, W.V., *Karl Rahner*, Collegeville, MN: The Liturgical Press, 1992.

Flannery, A., gen. ed., *Vatican Council II*. Boston, MA: St. Paul Editions - Daughters of St. Paul, 1988, Revised Edition.

Jeremias, J., *The Eucharistic Words of Jesus*. Philadelphia, PA: Fortress Press, 1986.

Kolatch, A., *The Jewish Book of Why*. Middle Village, NY: Jonathan David Publishers, Inc., 1995.

Komonchak, J.M., D. Collins, M. Lane, eds., *The New Dictionary of Theology*. Wilmington, DE: Glazier, 1989.

Manelli, S., *Jesus Our Eucharistic Love*. New Bedford, MA: Academy of the Immaculate, 1996.

Meyendorff, J., *Byzantine Theology*. New York: Fordham University Press, 1987.

Milavec, A., *The Didache*. New York/Mahwah, NJ: The Newman Press, 2003.

Murphy-O'Connor, J., *1 Corinthians*. Collegeville, MN: Michael Glazier, 1991.

Noll, R.R., *Christian Ministerial Priesthood*. San Francisco, CA: Catholic Scholars Press, 1993.

O'Connor, J.T., *The Hidden Manna*. San Francisco, CA: Ignatius Press, 2005.

Osborne, K., *Priesthood*. Mahwah, NJ: Paulist Press, 1989.

_____. *The Christian Sacraments of Initiation*. New York/ Mahwah, NJ: Paulist Press, 1987.

_____. *Ministry*. New York/Mahwah, NJ: Paulist Press, 2003.

Patrinacos, N., *A Dictionary of Greek Orthodoxy*. Pleasantville, NY: Hellenic Heritage Publications, 1987.

_____. *The Orthodox Liturgy*. Garwood, NJ: Graphic Arts Press, 1974.

# Bibliography

Pelikan, J., *The Christian Tradition*, Vol. I, *The Emergence of the Catholic Tradition* (100-600), Chicago, IL: University of Chicago Press, 1971.

_____. Vol. II, *The Spirit of Eastern Christendom* (600-1700). Chicago, IL: University of Chicago Press, 1978.

_____. *Whose Bible Is It?* New York: Penguin Group, 2005.

Rahner, K., *Theological Investigations*, Vol. V, Baltimore, MD: Helicon Press, 1963.

_____. *Foundations of Christian Faith*, New York: Crossroad, 1990.

Ratzinger, J., *God is Near Us.* San Francisco, CA: Ignatius Press, 2003.

Richardson, C., ed. *Early Christian Fathers.* New York: Macmillan Publishing Co., 1970.

Rordorf, W., et al, *The Eucharist of the Early Christians.* New York: Pueblo Publishing Company, 1978.

Schmemann, A., *The Eucharist.* Crestwood, NY: St. Vladimir's Seminary Press, 1988.

Vonier, A., *A Key to the Doctrine of the Eucharist.* Bethesda, MD: Zachaeus Press, 2003.

Ware, K.T., *The Orthodox Church.* New York: Penguin Books, 1982.

_____. *The Orthodox Way.* Crestwood, NY: St. Vladimir's Seminary Press, 1986.

_____. *Mary Theotokos in the Orthodox Tradition.* Wallington, Surrey, England: The Ecumenical Society of the Blessed Virgin Mary, 1997.

Zizioulas, J.T., *Being as Communion.* Crestwood, NY: St. Vladimir's Seminary Press, 2002.

_____. *Eucharist, Bishop, Church.* Brookline, MA: Holy Cross Orthodox Press, 2001.

## Articles, Papers, Lectures, Meetings

*America.* New York, NY: April 18, 2005.

Gerakas, A., "Karl Rahner & Grace," unpublished paper, 1993.

_____. "Diaconate — Its Dynamic Role in the Catholic Church," Dissertation, San Francisco Theological Seminary, Graduate Theological Union, 1996.

_____. "Orthodox Church, Baptism-Chrismation-Eucharist, A Comparison," unpublished paper, 2004.

_____. "Eucharist/Unity/Mary," unpublished paper, March, 1990.

John Paul II, *Orientale Lumen, The Light of the East.* Apostolic Letter, Boston, MA: Pauline Books & Media, 1995.

_____. *Ut Unum Sint.* Encyclical Letter, Boston, MA: Pauline Books & Media, 1995.

_____. *Ecclesia De Eucharistia.* Encyclical Letter, Rome: 2003.

_____. *Mane Nobiscum Domine.* For the Year of the Eucharist, Rome, 2004.

O'Collins, G., Lecture, Christology…, University of San Francisco, July 8, 1992.

O' Connor, J.M., Meeting, University of San Francisco, 23 June 1993.

*Orthodox Observer.* New York, NY: January, 2005; March 15-April 15, 2005.

*The Filioque: A Church-Dividing Issue?* An Agreed Statement of the North American Orthodox-Catholic Theological Consultation, USCCB, 2003.

*The National Herald.* Long Island City, NY: July 3-4, 2004.

ST PAULS

This book was produced by St. Pauls/Alba House, the Society of St. Paul, an international religious congregation of priests and brothers dedicated to serving the Church through the communications media.

For information regarding this and associated ministries of the Pauline Family of Congregations, write to the Vocation Director, Society of St. Paul, P.O. Box 189, 9531 Akron-Canfield Road, Canfield, Ohio 44406-0189. Phone (330) 702-0396; or E-mail: spvocationoffice@aol.com or check our internet site, www.albahouse.org